NORTH END BAPTIST CHURCH
7360 N. Clio Road
Mt. Morris, MI 48458
Phone number: (810) 687-2880
Website: www.northendbc.com

Sunrise IN A *Lemon* SKY

E. J. GORDON

E. J. Gordon
September 5, 2014

CROSSBOOKS

CrossBooks™
A Division of LifeWay
One LifeWay Plaza
Nashville, TN 37234
www.crossbooks.com
Phone: 1-866-768-9010

© 2014 E. J. Gordon. All rights reserved.

No part of this book may be reproduced, stored in a retrieval system, or transmitted by any means without the written permission of the author.

Scripture taken from the King James Version of the Bible.

First published by CrossBooks 7/15/2014

ISBN: 978-1-4627-3889-2 (sc)
ISBN: 978-1-4627-3890-8 (hc)
ISBN: 978-1-4627-3888-5 (e)

Library of Congress Control Number: 2014911569

Printed in the United States of America.

This book is printed on acid-free paper.

Any people depicted in stock imagery provided by Thinkstock are models, and such images are being used for illustrative purposes only. Certain stock imagery © Thinkstock.

Because of the dynamic nature of the Internet, any web addresses or links contained in this book may have changed since publication and may no longer be valid. The views expressed in this work are solely those of the author and do not necessarily reflect the views of the publisher, and the publisher hereby disclaims any responsibility for them.

Dedication

<u>Sunrise in a Lemon Sky</u> is dedicated to my sons, brother, cousins, professional colleagues, fellow writers, and kinfolk, all of whom may be cringing at the candor of this memoir.

To my precious girlfriends, you all know I would not be standing were it not for you.

Multiple preachers enriched my spiritual growth and I am grateful to them for pushing the envelope with me, for ministering to my needs, and sharing their faith. Their ministries encouraged me, challenged my thought, and opened my eyes and heart to God's personal touch and direction in my life.

Health care professionals deserve far more than a dedication line as their actions combined with God's healing mercy and grace saved my life.

I further dedicate this book to the man who turned my world "outside-in" and upside-down, the man in my path when I needed him. I tripped over my own feet and into his open arms.

Perhaps it is only when we come to terms with life's fragile nature that we truly begin to live.

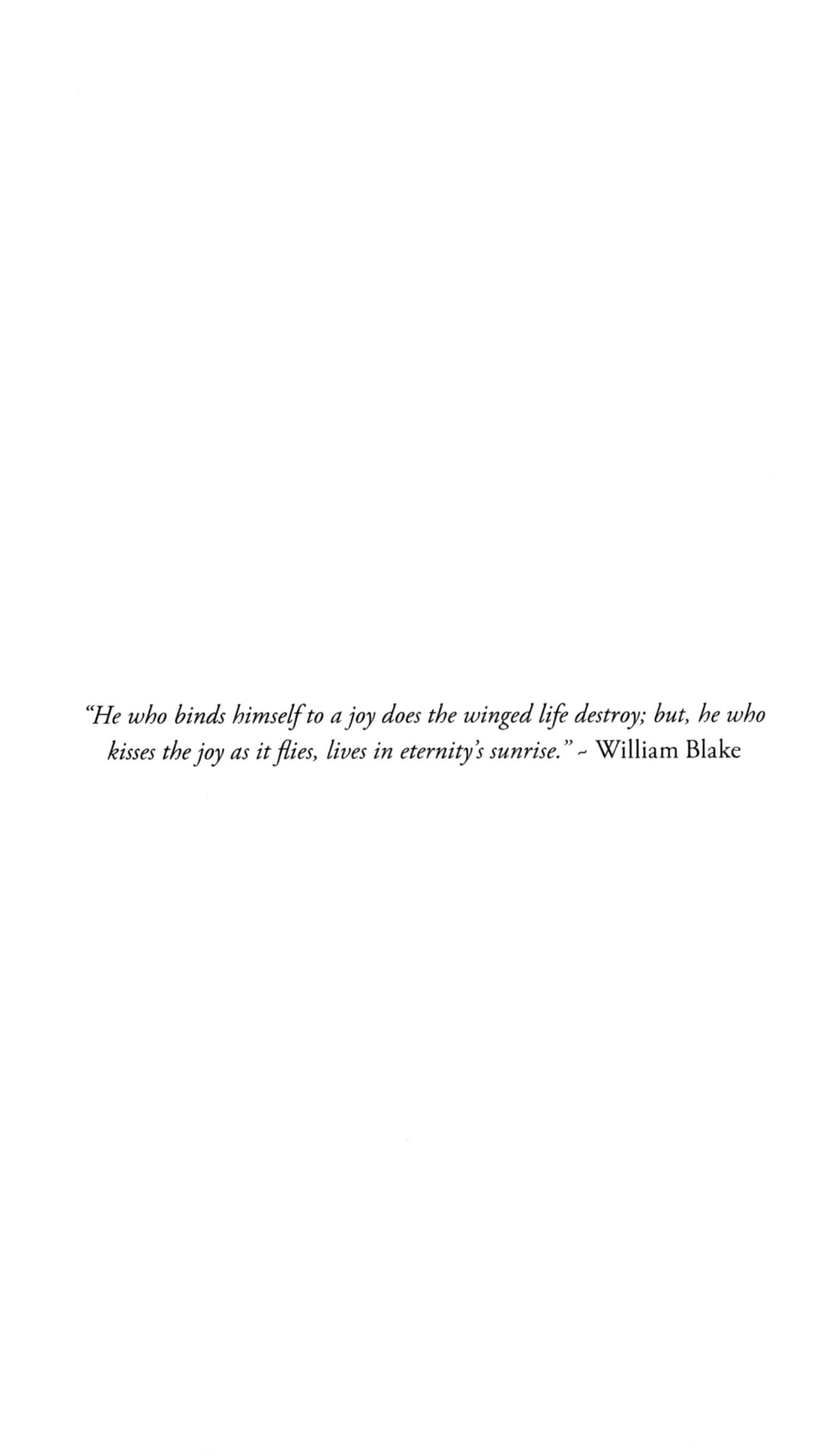

"He who binds himself to a joy does the winged life destroy; but, he who kisses the joy as it flies, lives in eternity's sunrise." ~ William Blake

Contents

Preface xi
Introduction xiii

Chapter 1   I'll Have What She's Having 1
Chapter 2   When You Least Expect It 11
Chapter 3   Stay Up and Fight or Go to Bed Mad 17
Chapter 4   Let Me Count the Ways 25
Chapter 5   Going to the Mattresses: Fight for Survival 31
Chapter 6   You Can-Survive 47
Chapter 7   Chainsaw Massacre 53
Chapter 8   You Ignorant Slut 59
Chapter 9   Birthday Reality 67
Chapter 10   Big Bad Wolf Insurance 73
Chapter 11   Waiting for the Next Mr. Wrong 79
Chapter 12   Dancing With Frogs 89
Chapter 13   Carousel Ride 95
Chapter 14   Roadmaps, Roadblocks, and Stop Signs 101
Chapter 15   Sweeter than Wine 107
Chapter 16   My Love Story 113
Chapter 17   It Was All So Subtle 119
Chapter 18   Life's Tapestry Unravels 129
Chapter 19   Holding On or Letting Go 137
Chapter 20   "Marriage is not for me." 145

Conclusion 151
Epilogue 159
Index to "Food for Thought" 161
About the Author 165

Preface

Writers must write. Within me lived a series of stories of survival on many levels. I began to see the common thread in each story. Not that God caused any of the events, but His hand guided me through each trial to a monumental chorus of "Hallelujah!"

Write it, OK. But why publish it? In the midst of my struggle for help and direction, I found books with quick-fixes, advising me to "do this or that to remedy your situation."

Sometimes good intentioned people told me to own my situation and discover a panacea through almonds, ginger, or internet research. My mother convinced me to drink Lydia Pinkham's tonic, a concoction for whatever ails women. At other junctures, I was serenaded with "don't worry – be happy." The worst suggestion: let go and let God. Only Little Miss Muffet sits on her tuffet, eating truffles, running away at the slightest hint of trouble. None of these snippets is worth squat. Maybe there's something else.

I did wonder why all these situations were coming my way, one right after another. Some might say that God insisted I face them as a way of teaching me lessons. Others could believe that God desired to prove He is stronger than anything that could come my way and he wanted to humble me. I don't believe the purpose was any of these things, though each outcome occurred.

Watershed events, trials, and earth-shaking situations happen in every person's life. Here's the truth: I did not know that. I believed that if I played fair, was a good girl, obeyed all the rules of civilized behavior, loved God and believed in His Son Jesus Christ, I would be spared the pings and dents, the hammered consequences that result from acting with no regard for the rules. If one truth supersedes, it is this: I played by the rules.

Therefore, when unexplained challenges came, when my sky fell, I tumbled from a lofty pedestal of my own creation.

This book refused to stay unwritten. "You could write a book," friends would tell me. Then, "You should write a book. Others might be encouraged, or they might avoid some of the turmoil you experienced." Finally, "You must write a book. People need to see God's hand in your life. You could make a real difference in someone's life. Let them know they are not alone."

Many opportunities to abandon the project came along. Self-doubt, fear of recrimination, and the thought that some might consider the book a published pity-party have stymied me from time to time. With every moment of hesitancy, I have gone back to the manuscript and considered modifications that would continue to tell the truth, but share the story in a different manner.

As I began to write the various stories, I wrote as catharsis. The tone in some sections was unhealthy and heavily sarcastic, too weepy in others. I began to revise with the goal of releasing the energy for the purpose of good for others and for me. The goal of this book, therefore, is to get the story told and for women to experience encouragement in the various trials they are facing. The tone is authentic, not saccharine.

I learned the meaning of Longfellow's line from his rhyming *Psalm of Life*: "Act-act in the Living Present; Heart within and God overhead."

In addition, I hope to give a nod to romance and help women navigate the path to a new beginning. And in all of it, my wish is to honor God's hand at work in my life.

Introduction

Taste of Lemons

Don't stand there and tell me you didn't see it coming. There are always clues. Hoping that the whole thing will go away, how is that a strategy? As Dr. Phil would say, "How's that working for you?"

I'm telling you, I never saw any of it coming. Peyton Manning, quarterback legend in the NFL, claims he can sense it coming. Leigh Anne Tuohy and Michael Oher gained recognition with the phrase from her book and the subsequent semi-biographical movie, <u>The Blind Side</u> (Alcon Entertainment and Warner Bros. Pictures). Unlike seasoned quarterbacks who dodge oncoming linebackers, I did not side-step anything. The blind side got me good. Here I stand, though, wishing to share insights through my story.

Perhaps after reading <u>Sunrise in a Lemon Sky</u>, more people will be able to recognize the shaking earth beneath their feet for what it is. They will be able to sense calamity's thunderous approach as it prepares to create havoc, to blindside. The sunrises contained here, supplying the title for the book, are both blinding and hopeful; the taste of the lemon, both tart and sweet.

Current self-help books do not address what I consider to be the straight, hard truth: people's lives are in crisis, dysfunction swirls around us, fallout drifts upon us like soot; nothing short of miracles can rescue these families. The puzzling origin of traumas which arrive unannounced at our doorstep defies reason. Ask, "Why?" all day long. There is no answer. So, the question follows, "From where will the courage come to see it, face it, act on it, and survive?"

In writing <u>Sunrise in a Lemon Sky</u>, I am able to share experiences that nearly took me to the grave and did take me to my knees. I hope to share the miraculous dichotomy of loss resulting in gain, last becoming first, accepting what was once rejected, allowing God to illuminate a path once thought impossible to navigate.

In the following pages I've shared stories told from my perspective. My story is not comprised of the worst circumstances in life, by any means. The circumstances were the worst for me, though, and they beg to be told. You might be exactly the one who needs to read it. Someone might shrug and think, "I've known worse." That's the way life goes. What can I say?

It has taken over nineteen years to write this book, the last seven years spent penning it, revising it, and finding the right voice to express the message. Praise God that I am alive to share my journey with you.

> *By reading <u>Sunrise in a Lemon Sky</u>, you will share experiences that nearly took me to the grave and did take me to my knees.*

The joy that has come continues as a daily gift. What God has done for me, He will gladly do for anyone willing to surrender, pray and ask. You must, too, be willing to act.

Please read the quotes and scriptures found in the **Reflection** sections: be active in reflection. Consider purchasing a *Reflection Journal*, or notebook. When a person writes, thought becomes authentic.

Enjoy the recipes and anecdotes I have included: **Food for Thought**. Consider how cooking builds relationships and how lessons learned in the kitchen translate into our culture. Biblical truths comprise the paramount reason for including the recipes. Romans 8:28 (KJV) - "And we know that all things work together for good to them that love God, to them who are the called according to his purpose." Ingredients taken individually are tasteless or even bitter. But, when combined (working together) and fired correctly, the combination is delicious (good). So, too, is life. **When you begin to count your losses, instead, count what you have gained!**

INTRODUCTION – Taste of Lemons - Food for Thought:

Here is the first recipe. Enjoy *"Mother's Easy Pound Cake."*

MOTHER'S EASY POUND CAKE

It took years for me to perfect this recipe. Make it exactly as the recipe indicates. Use only the specified ingredients, unless you are adventuresome in baking. Mix in the specific order given and beat the mixture between each addition. If you don't do this, the recipe will self-destruct. She named it "Easy" Pound Cake, because it was easy for her! Once, as a young girl, I dumped all the ingredients into one bowl, cranked up the mixer, and Voila! I baked something akin to a pound cake, but it was a distant flat and heavy cousin. Without mixing between ingredients, you will create a flop.

2 stick oleo (not butter, actually- only use Kroger or Imperial brand margarine)	Cream butter and sugar using the mixer.
2 cups sugar	3 eggs – then beat the mixture

Add 1 cup *WR* (best choice) – not bread flour- and beat
Add 3 more eggs and beat
Add 1 more cup *WR* (good stuff) flour and beat more
Add 2 tsp vanilla (Mexican)
Beat again and then add 1 tsp almond extract
Bake in greased and floured Bundt pan at 350 degrees for 55 minutes (watch it when it begins to smell delicious).
Do not overbake.

Mother-in-Law "outside-in" CAKE recipe:

1 box butter pecan cake mix (Betty Crocker, Duncan Hines)	1 cup water 4 eggs ¾ cup oil

Save for later: *1 container coconut pecan frosting (Betty Crocker, Duncan Hines)*
Mix cake mix, water, eggs, and Oil
Beat on Medium High for two minutes
<u>Slowly</u> *stir in frosting. Do not beat, just gently stir.*
Pour mixture into prepared Bundt pan
Bake at 350 degrees for 45 min.
Do not overbake.
Turn out of pan.
This cake is better after a day to "set" and become moist.

CHAPTER 1

I'll Have What She's Having

Locked away in her vast storehouse of Reputation Rules, she'd find the answer. She was the keeper of the keys.

"Mother, let me ask you something."

We sat at the kitchen table that December morning after I spent a weekend at a college girlfriend's house. My heartthrob and I had found ways to be alone. Lights low, soft couch, Lover-boy and I ventured into a breathless make-out session. I was asking permission (or forgiveness) to go forward; Mother could always provide chapter and verse.

"Mother, is it okay to kiss while in a reclining position?"

I actually said that. Her answer, combined with the teachings of Ann Landers, encouraged me to keep my knees pressed firmly together and keep one foot on the floor.

Women's magazines, cinema, television, and novels of all genres contain at least a perfunctory nod to sex, sexual satisfaction, and sexy photographs. While heavy emphasis on all things sexual is somewhat current, the focus on personal satisfaction for both men and women had its fledgling years. Dating, engagement, and marriage for me happened in my awakening decades, with sex education taught by Ann Landers.

The night before my wedding, Mother turned the tables and posed a question to me.

"Do you have anything you want to talk about or ask?"

If I had asked one question about what I really did not know, I thought I would have embarrassed myself and her so much that I doubt the conversation could have progressed. She asked out of motherly obligation. I knew what she meant.

I said, "No."

In retrospect, she could have shared much that I needed to hear. The question came, however, a little late. The next day was D-Day.

As she had never made this kind of overture, I was taken aback and felt uncomfortable engaging in a conversation about what I could expect in the bedroom. I wish that my mother and I had kept an ongoing, open communication link about all things womanly. Since the piece of conflicting advice about keeping my knees together and one foot on the floor, I figured no useful tidbit would come from a conversation about sex, wedded or otherwise. We just didn't talk about it. If we had been honest, her insights along the way could have saved us both a great deal of heartache.

I had lived in an apartment with three other girls and had worked six months in a large city before marrying. We girls engaged in some lusty conversations, but only one of us was experienced, and we let her believe we knew it all, too.

> *Lectures at the feet of my mother assured me that one moment of illicit pleasure would be paid for with a walk down the aisle in an off-white wedding gown.*

I knew next to nothing about being a grown-up woman. But, one night in that apartment, I read portions of *The Joy of Sex* and gaped at the pictures. I confess I had to close the book from time to time because I wondered, "Who are the men and women who do that?" All I learned regarding womanly sex education was through conversation with other women, many as naïve as I.

I had to trust that my future husband would take the lead in our love life. He would have to usher me into self-discovery and the pleasure of married love. As a young woman, I had erected a monumental wall, guarded day and night, to preserve my reputation.

During dating and engagement periods, I had kept one foot on the floor and the other on the brake. Guys respected my limits. As required by holy law and family decree, I intended to go to my wedding bed a virgin. Regardless of how many of us were left to participate in The Parade, my understanding of the rules was explicit.

In fairness, neither he nor I was educated in the joy of sex. As for my part, I simply had no womanly knowledge or courage. I had longings and ideas for after marriage but no gumption to explore further. Instilled in me deeply was the requirement of a good reputation and biblical obedience. I believed that should virginity be surrendered prior to marriage, I'd be shamed, my family humiliated, and I'd be relegated to the off-white wedding dress.

Imagine the conversation with the bridal consultant: "Are you pure as the driven snow, my dear?" She summons Heather Prynne to cloak me in scarlet, affixing a cluster of A's to my bodice should I utter the unthinkable answer.

"Oh, well, (tsk-tsk), let's go into the section for girls like you. These dresses are designed in off-white, ecru, and cream. I'm sure you'll look radiant (eyes rolling) in one of these."

Lectures at the feet of my mother assured me that one moment of illicit pleasure would be paid for with a walk down the aisle in an off-white wedding gown. Gasps of disbelief would ripple through the pews as the blemished bride moved toward the groom, her reputation to be sacrificed on the altar of back-fence gossip.

Mother of All Mothers ran serious boyfriends through the Junior League pre-nuptial testing center and awarded a blue ribbon for good news or no news in the family lineage category, ribbons like a pig earns at the county fair. She could take to her bed for whatever length of time necessary for my behavior to correct itself. She controlled my journeys into experimentation with abundant helpings of guilt, though we were not related to Barbra Streisand.

Ridiculous as that imaginary bridal consultant conversation may be, the preservation of virginity prior to the wedding night was of paramount importance, both in church and in family. My groom-to-be was raised with the same understanding. An imaginary piece of white foam held firmly between the knees, served as the only birth control pill I needed. The Mother Rules were biblical. Girls like me wondered, dreamed, hoped, and blushed.

He was a charmer and I did love him. He was sometimes the kindest gentlemen during our romance. He courted me with letters, gifts, flowers, music; when we broke up during that time period, we'd reattach after he wrote letters begging forgiveness and explaining the blunder of stomping all over my heart. He pled, "What would my life be without you?" We were meant for each other.

At times, he was a total jackass and patterns of behavior surfaced that became too prevalent. These were the warnings that I ignored. These incidents were forgiven. I was convinced it would be true love forever.

In marriage, he led me into our intimate relations and was thoughtful, kind, and sensitive. In fairness, I do not know if my psyche would have allowed for fiery passion at that time. I'll never know. What I never knew, I would never miss. Until later.

My libido awakened several years later than most. The older we became and the more aware I grew of my own sensuality, the more intimate a connection I craved. That awakening should have been the most freeing experience a husband and wife can share: discovering the passion of married love within the privacy and sanctity of the marriage bed. At that juncture, however, he spent more energy in pursuit of a promising career.

Credit my awakening to a maturing psyche, conversations with friends about date night, and self-help paperbacks in the guise of racy romance novels. I wanted what everyone else was having: passion and sexual satisfaction with my husband. Was that possible, or was it fabricated by someone with an active imagination and a publishing contract? Must have been fantasy, I surmised. I needed to get into the real world and forget about passion found only in the movies and brown paper-wrapped cult fiction.

I knew fairly early that something vital to my happiness was missing from our marriage. This man, however, was a gentleman, a professional, and he had many honorable qualities. I was charmed with how witty he was and how smart. We made a good team and presented an image of a modern American couple. Therefore, I set aside the signs that our personal needs were not the same.

> *After all, marriage is not all about sex. But it should be about sex some of the time, don't you think?*

I barely knew what my needs or expectations were at that time in my life, but I did know that he did not show me he loved me as much as I needed. I needed words and touch and recognized it long before the book on love languages was written. I longed for the security of physical and emotional contact. "I need you to hold me, kiss me, shower me with affection designed only for me."

He told me I should quit focusing on myself and turn my focus to others. "I'm not your babysitter. I am not in charge of your happiness. You are capable of taking care of yourself. Surely you are not that needy." The more I expressed my need, the more guilt he served. I felt guilty for wanting to be cherished and cared for. I was thinking too much of myself.

"You are the unhappiest person I know. I can't make you happy. Happiness comes from within. Selfishness spawns unhappiness. Grow up."

I did not recognize the woman he described. I was happy. I wanted him to show me how much he loved me. While it is important for happiness to bubble from within, and no one can *make* anyone else happy, it would be wonderful if I felt he would go out of his way to see me smile, just for him. I wanted to feel that I was the center of his universe, that he loved me beyond measure. He let me believe that request was ridiculous and juvenile. It hurt for him to say I should "get over it."

In our exclusive love life, without children for ten years, we should have been enjoying each other more than we did. He could send a smile my way, capture my eyes and my heart, and lead me to emotional intimacy. I did not try any womanly come-ons at this juncture; I felt self-conscious. I came to believe that my expectations were unrealistic. After all, marriage is not all about sex. But it should be about sex some of the time, don't you think?

From what I experienced, my advice is this: if you doubt your emotional needs will be met, take action and move on. Believe in your own worth enough to insist that your needs be acknowledged and met. As women, we set our needs aside for others but a lifetime of that behavior is unhealthy. We've made our choices but to lie in that made bed is not always the answer.

I am aware that marriage is not a constant honeymoon. If, however, a person is thirsty and finds no water and continues to search and still finds none, the lack of water and the search for it become an obsession. Everything is affected by the lack of water and the quest becomes the person's singular focus.

A person can be happy if every need is not met. That's maturity: real life. God gave me plenty of happiness and I am grateful. I craved intimacy, the touch of my husband's hand, the physical contact. My self-respect became fragile and damaged. Issues left unresolved continued because I accepted the behaviors that undermined my ego.

Here is the good news: God will not give up trying to save you from yourself. God leads, answers prayer, speaking directly to His people. God provides not only better than we deserve, but He gives us what we need when we did not realize how desperately we needed it. It's hard to see this fact when covered with the fall-out of a troubled marriage. You should be prepared to follow God's lead and walk where you did not know you wanted to go.

Follow my story into the early years, as I stumble along rocky pathways.

Chapter 1 - I'll Have What She's Having - Reflection:

You married him. You were content enough and enjoyed your relationship enough to marry him, and he, you. If you have young children, it's best to think about the long range consequences of divorce.

What will your children say, and what will you think 20 years down the road? There must be more serious thought to such a decision, such as marital counseling, conscious decision to spend more "quality time together," etc. Age plays a huge role in a decision such as the one you might be contemplating. Think, seriously.

Think about your expectation regarding intimacy within marriage. If any of these quotes relate to your understanding of your own needs, desires, or expectations, try to put those desires into words. If not, create your own written expectation of your intimate time within your marriage.

1. "I don't know the question, but sex is definitely the answer."
   — Woody Allen

2. "We waste time looking for the perfect lover, instead of creating the perfect love." Tom Robbins

3. "Sex without love is as hollow and ridiculous as love without sex." Hunter S. Thompson

Tart lesson: Sometimes, you cannot have it all.   *Sweet treat: But, sometimes, you can.*

Chapter 1 - I'll Have What She's Having - Food for Thought:

Disasters in the kitchen, such as the one recounted with Mother's Easy Pound Cake, are due to inexperience. "Just stop." That was Mother's primary remark. "I'll do it." So, my neighborhood friend and I, in *her* mother's kitchen, made enough biscuit dough for a hotel. We got our hands on the wrong recipe and into dough expanding enough to feed the multitude. At about age ten, I perked instant coffee to surprise Mother and Daddy with breakfast. Not being able to find the regular coffee and thinking all coffee the same, I filled the percolator with Maxwell House Instant Coffee. Daddy appreciated my efforts. I'll stop there.

    Before I married, rather than conduct a frank and forthcoming discussion about marriage expectations, Mother determined it was time I learned to cook. I was recording some of her recipes and asking questions. I drew pictures of a colander and a boiler. No one should be surprised. Inexperience in all aspects brought into a marriage should be addressed fully, whether it's cooking or sex.

This recipe has been in my family for generations. I share it in the way that I wish my mother had shared what she knew and believed about love, her relationships, and her life-long love for my father and their 50+ year marriage. She kept her kitchen expertise to herself as she kept her personal story.

Date-nut Cake

1 c butter	2 pkg dates
2 c sugar	1 qt pecans – small pieces
2 ½ c flour	1 t baking powder
7 eggs-separated	1 tumbler good brandy (optional)

Cream butter and sugar, add egg yolks one at a time, alternating with flour. Add beaten egg whites, dates, and nuts which have been cut into small pieces. Bake in large loaf pan or bundt pan for 2 ½ hours at 300 degrees.

Chapter 2

When You Least Expect It

At each milestone, each Christmas, every New Year, even at the yearly car inspections with the dated reminder sticker, I prayed that I might become pregnant by the next landmark event. Of course, I did not see God's plan in the midst of that disappointment.

When friends called to share that they were pregnant, I gave the performance of a lifetime, an Oscar nomination. One sweet friend called to cry on my shoulder over an unexpected pregnancy. After the conversation, I threw myself atop my bed, like a teenager, and wept for myself. God was at work, though. I learned that. He knew what I needed and what would be best for me.

Remaining without children in a child-filled world created a deep longing for years, but His answer fulfilled my dreams. It came from nothing I had ever planned. The story is a beautiful testament to God's activity in our lives.

As years went by and I did not conceive, for mysterious and puzzling reasons, I began to wonder what was wrong with me. He agreed to the sperm mobility/motility test, vitality test, and I had my tubes opened and a D&C performed, to ease conception. I visited a fertility specialist who gave me the classic advice: calm down. "When you least expect it" is ridiculous when I am expectant at every moment of every day.

It is challenging what couples endure in order to conceive when the routine followed by most couples does not produce a baby. There's heartache, disappointment and disillusionment when pregnancy does not happen. Home remedies such as Lydia Pinkham's tonic claiming "a baby in every bottle" I guzzled. It tasted worse than NyQuil and no baby was in any of the bottles I drank. So, with help from the gynecologist writing a prescription for fertility pills, I was encouraged and cautioned.

Some church-going, good-intentioned ladies advised me to get right with God. They believed I had done something sinister, something akin to worshiping a golden calf, which would keep my womb closed, a curse from Old Testament. With hips raised to the heavens in hopes of a miracle opening, I tried it all.

Then, I felt defeated when I spent months with temperature charts and the fertility drug Clomid only to be turned away at the perfect time of the month. The fun couples are supposed to experience conceiving a baby turned into work. As Scarlett would say with disdain, "Fun! Fiddle-dee-dee!"

Risks with fertility drugs are hefty, but if a couple is desirous of a child, risk is taken. I was taking the drugs, taking the health risk. I'd take my temperature before my feet hit the floor every morning. I'd chart the reading, make the graph, calculate the monthly pattern, circle the date with times prior to ovulation and just after. Movies depicting a husband rushing home to meet the appointed hour are not exaggerations. We had agreed. This would be our way of conception. I did my part, I believed. Work with me here.

> *I do not believe that I am the puppet master directing the Almighty God with prayer: give me a baby and a parking place at the front door of Wal-Mart.*

The frequency that is needed to conceive became a chore. He dreaded the time when I slithered into the den in my black slinky with notice that it was now time to have sex. He felt called upon to perform, an obligation that was a turn-off. From what I have read over the course of many years, keeping all parties sexy, interested, and performing when the thermometer says "it's time" is precarious. I did not do a very good job of any of it. Many opportunities to conceive were missed. That compounded my belief that I was not feminine enough, sexy enough, woman enough in my marriage.

Let's just say that while I was praying for a child, God knew I'd have children, but not in the manner I thought. I do not believe that I am the puppet master directing the Almighty God with prayer: give me a baby and a parking place at the front door of Wal-Mart. But, I do believe that God is interested in the intricacies of life. The book entitled *A Baby, Maybe* encouraged me to see my life as "child-free" rather than "child-less." Interesting point: one I never embraced.

God gave me children. The children are divine gifts, through adoption, born not from my womb, but from within my heart.

Little did I know at the time that God's plan for my life and for theirs was wonderful. His plan for these boys was that I would be their mother. They were not aborted. Their biological mothers decided, or God decided for them, that the child each conceived would live. Each player in these children's lives followed a God-directed path to a Christian adoption agency.

The experience with that agency was a remarkable one in how the social workers and adoption counselors grew us as perspective parents. The twelve–fourteen month process placed just the right baby with just the right parents. Their decisions as well as ours were inspired by God.

Our second son was placed with us by the adoption counselor who arrived after a troubled time within the agency. She found our application packet for a second child in the bottom of a file cabinet, covered with miscellaneous paperwork. We had abandoned all hope by the time she called us.

"Your baby has been born," she informed us after an update of our file and an extensive home visit. Within two weeks, we brought our second son home. Ours was the only placement she made, as she was needed at another agency in another city. God brought her to our baby and our baby to us. I have not the words to convey how great is our God.

I am reminded of a sermon I heard recently: Moses' mother, in order to give him life and save him from certain death at the hands of the Egyptians, gave him up. She placed him in the basket of straw and mud, made safe by her hands joined with God. She set him afloat, pushed him into that river, praying that he would be found by someone in the palace of the Pharaoh. She could not have known that the daughter of Pharaoh would be the one to find him, and could not have imagined she would then send for a nurse from among the Hebrew women. And, isn't God able to work it out; it was Moses' own mother who was selected to nurse and raise him for the daughter of Pharaoh. How God does work his miracles for His glory and for our good, when we have no knowledge of what His overall plan might be. We can only trust that God has different plans for us, perhaps better than we could ever imagine.

We completed a family through adoption. He gave us the children He wanted us to have in the time frame He chose, and through a process I had never considered. Opening doors along another hallway in a wing of life I had not envisioned fulfilled my deep longing to be a mother. These children: I could not be more grateful.

The moment a baby is placed into the arms of his mother, he is affixed permanently into her heart. As fulfilling as the experience of growing a child within your own body must be, those nine months represent but a fraction of time relative to the eternity of motherhood.

Today, international adoptions, open adoptions, and private adoptions are restrained by extensive paperwork, legal wrangling, and money. Still, God works in the lives of people who have a heart for parenting. God leads. We act.

How limited in vision must be the eyes of those who define motherhood in one way only. It happened, just not the way I thought it would. Isn't God so like that? My world expanded to the moon and back, as did my heart.

Chapter 2 – When You Least Expect It - Reflection:

Respond to this quote: "If you want to be reminded of the love of the Lord, just watch the sunrise." — Jeannette Walls, *Half Broke Horses*

God through Jesus experienced the human condition. So many times we say, "God knows, I have tried." Write what the phrase "God Knows" means to you.

Take a few moments and list what **God Knows** about you, about who you are and what you believe. Write about the experiences you've had that only God knows. What does God know about wrongs you have committed, about the wrongs committed against you?

List the benefits you have received from God, benefits that are His design and not yours.

Tart Lesson: When God whispers, listen.   Sweet Pleasure: You can have your dream, God's way.

Chapter 2 – When You Least Expect It - Food for Thought:

My sons enjoy the family movie, *A Christmas Story*. The *Fable of the Leg Lamp* might be an apt title, for people usually remember that garish symbol in the family's living room window. They remember also the putrid pink bunny suit that Ralphie had to model. My boys like the scenes about food, such as the scene at the supper table: a staple of meat loaf and mashed potatoes with Randy eating only if challenged to eat like a piggy. Our most hilarious memory takes us to the "open on Christmas Day" Peking-duck restaurant where dinner is served after the hounds have devoured the family's Christmas turkey. "Fa Ra Ra Ra Ra…" Bring down the meat cleaver upon the neck of the smiling duck and the boys dissolve into laughter. What a joyous sound, even now.

My sons' favorite breakfast treat is French toast. We cover both sides of the toast with cinnamon-sugar, blended at home. It was one of my delights as a child, also, so the French toast breakfast scene in *Kramer vs Kramer* was poignant. One disastrous morning, newly separated Dustin Hoffman awakes to his new reality and makes breakfast with his adorable son. The French toast probably won't be that bad, but the question, "You like crunchy French toast?" says a lot.

The sounds of our children's laughter, memories of making breakfast together, what could ever be more important than family?

Magic Meat Loaf

1– 2lbs ground chuck
1 ½ t salt and pepper
1 egg, beaten
½ pkg frozen onion & green pepper pieces
¼ c crushed crackers

Sauce: 8 oz tomato sauce with seasoning of your choice (for meat loaf, or sauce with onion and peppers)

½ - ¾ c brown sugar (to your taste) 1 t mustard

Use ½ sauce in mixing the meat loaf and ½ sauce on top
Bake at 375 degrees for 45 min to 1 hour. Use the special meat loaf pan that traps the grease below.

Chapter 3

Stay Up and Fight or Go to Bed Mad

Instead of a nightgown, I should have donned battle gear.

"We need to talk," I said.

"What about?" He was clueless.

At first, I was historical.

That changed to hysterical somewhere around midnight.

The 10PM-2AM discussions dissolved into all-night sessions. The garbage of the past months was dumped upon the bed.

Being non-confrontational and very sensitive to criticism, I kept to myself all the injuries until I could take it no more.

If I called attention to a situation or a hurt, I would discover that the blame lay at my feet. He could turn the discussion on a dime and was well-practiced. I'd rather keep silent than feel the blame when he'd turn the tables and indicate that the hurt was my fault.

I'd wither and be reborn as Evelyn Couch, cursing and driving with lots of insurance in *Fried Green Tomatoes at the Whistle Stop Cafe*. Unfounded accusations shocked me into aggression and loosed the lock on my words, and I'd counter with all the injustices I had stored up for the past whatever length of time. It was horribly unfair: all around.

I needed to learn how to let him know I was hurt without hurting him back. He needed to hear my hurt and respond without heaping the guilt on me. Neither of us knew that having a good knock-down-drag-out could be healthy, as long as no one is actually knocked down or drug out. The internal turmoil of holding back and keeping quiet was as destructive as the hurtful words. Conflict within marriage is natural. Who knew?

"Why stay up late making each other more miserable when you can get a good night's sleep and probably feel better in the morning?" Lydia Netzer said the same in her Blog post on *15 Ways to Stay Married for 15 Years* which circulated on the Internet.

It would have saved feelings had we set a time limit and gone to sleep. But, nobody does that. We never kissed and made up before we called a halt to the barbs, insults, hurtful truths. We would just get tired or he'd drop off to sleep and snore, and then we'd turn away from each other at 2 or 3 AM, and get over it the next day. Nothing was ever resolved, except a good airing out of injustices. The hurt was tangible.

> *Divorce might follow, but if not, misery surely will.*

A well-known comedienne Phyllis Diller shared her opinion: "Don't go to bed mad. Stay up and Fight!" More often than not, arguments happen in the evening when both people have come home from a tiring, stressful day at work. Add children to the mix and by a heavy silence, the couple agrees to skirmish once the kids are asleep. If the issue isn't resolved by bed time, the couple ends up going to bed angry. There's no resolution to the issue and words produce little more than additional anger.

The main point: work it out before 10PM. Let that be the goal. Agree to start early and work it out by 10PM. Sometimes, just agree to disagree and acknowledge that each heart is more important than hurt; saved feelings supersede either person being right. Both parties might practice "I'm Sorry. I love you. We'll get this resolved tomorrow, I promise."

Awake and angry, though, allows time to think of more reasons why you're right and your spouse is wrong, and all the ways he/she has wronged you since you said I do. Unload all the garbage onto the den floor and wrestle around in it there, rather than on your duvet cover. If the airing-out is going to take a while, find a time to halt, think on it until the next day. Desiring to fulfill the needs of the other must take center stage. If it's all about "my way," then it's all about the "highway," sooner or later.

Set ground rules. Decide on words that will never be used. Declare truce words or danger words. Do not fight with a trigger-happy partner who knows sensitive buttons and intends to push them all. I have never experienced anything good about an argument held in the late evening or just before bed, for the sake of not going to bed mad. Words from the scriptures suggest that we not let the sun go down on our anger. Check out the sun's location before you get anything started! In actuality, you need to voice the problem, and if it's not going to be solved quickly, calm down and sleep on it. Let each person try to come to terms with the situation and find within him/herself a way to have both people within the couple emerge unbruised.

I am certain that these battle situations did not improve anything in our marriage. We did not know how to fight fair. We did not know how to give each other what we needed in any way. We could talk about many topics, but not about ourselves. It took summonsing my courage to address any conflict. I'd put it off and off and off, knowing what most probably would be the result: a major gut-stomping session. So, I shoved my resentment down until it bubbled over and I ruined the evening, the day, the week, the month, whatever I'd been trying save.

Trying to make sense of the variances in our understandings and desires, both of us read Gail Sheehy's groundbreaking work, *Passages*, published in 1976. The book contains an overview of adulthood passages for men and women, couples and singles, as these stages have been explained for toddlers and teens. Still a marvelous textbook on the stages of adulthood, *Passages* and its more recent updates continues to be relevant. We discussed the book and its meaning for us. These discussions bridged some gaps in our relationship.

Within the mess resulting from unfulfilled needs, we carved out a niche of surface harmony, a couple of parenting roles, and a social persona. The emotional connection continued in its complicated pattern. What I needed and wanted within my marriage continued its elusive nature. We remained married. That is God's will. It was certainly my plan.

Chapter 3 – Stay Up and Fight or Go to Bed Mad - Reflection:

Respond to this quote: "There was never a night or a problem that could defeat sunrise or hope." - Bern Williams

List the mistakes discussed in this chapter and decide how you would correct them, or do something different.

What is your preference? "Stay up and fight" or "Go to bed mad." Explain.

"Every right implies a responsibility; every opportunity, an obligation, every possession, a duty." John D. Rockefeller

Read the following scripture. Next, write a personal reflection about the meaning of each scripture for your life.

Proverbs 15: 1*: A soft answer turneth away wrath: but grievous words stir up anger.*

Proverbs 15: 18 *A wrathful man stirreth up strife: but he that is slow to anger appeaseth strife.*

Chapter 3 – Stay Up and Fight or Go to Bed Mad
Food for Thought:

Recipe for the Perfect Marriage with comments by Red Skelton, comedian

1. If no pots and pans are "bucking" on the stove and there is no aroma of the usual delicious supper, suggest that you take her out to eat.
    Red Skelton: Two times a week, we go to a nice restaurant, have a little beverage, good food and companionship. She goes on Tuesdays, I go on Fridays.

2. Remember her birthday, your anniversary, all the holidays, and have a standing tab at the jeweler and the florist.
    Red Skelton: I asked my wife where she wanted to go for our anniversary. "Somewhere I haven't been in a long time!" she said. So I suggested the kitchen.

3. Don't ever threaten a separation, divorce, or leaving. Don't even allow such comments to come up in a heated exchange of ideas. Once it's out there, it's there.
    Red Skelton: Remember: Marriage is the number one cause of divorce.

4. Talk less; Listen more. Listen with your heart and your ears. "Last words" are sometimes just that.

   Red Skelton: I haven't spoken to my wife in 18 months. I don't like to interrupt her.

5. Go ahead and fight, but fight fair and both of you practice these words: "It was my fault and I'm sorry."

   Red Skelton: The last fight was my fault. My wife asked "What's on the TV?" I said "Dust!"

CHAPTER 4

Let Me Count the Ways

"Stop."

I moved my hand from his chest.

Propped on an elbow, a quizzical look helped form the question, I asked, "Why?"

He was silent, staring at the ceiling, hands folded across his chest.

"Your expectation of me is beyond what I can give you."

"Huh?"

"Just stop."

"I want you to love me and let me love you. What's so hard about that?"

"You don't understand what I'm saying to you. When you come toward me like that, when you expect me to respond, it's a demand and it turns me off. It's something else on your list."

"A demand?" I questioned.

"I shut down because I can't meet your level of expectation."

"Yes, you can."

"No, I can't."

From that impasse, I sat fully upright and listened. His litany of my shortcomings became more harsh. The words swirled in my mind, feeling alternately like fire and ice. I felt as if I'd been slapped, kicked, stomped with words, all belittling me as a woman, as a wife.

We had plowed through the muddy ground of conception on demand with dirt clods scattered across the bedroom. The plow lay idle in the barn. Though my gynecologist explained that no clinical reason existed for me not to become pregnant, I set aside that desire because I was mother to two marvelous sons. We did not need sex for procreation; we needed lovemaking. The relationship I craved with my husband was one of physical intimacy, regardless of any previous gymnastic obligations. I could not understand how loving could be a chore.

The memory of that night is emblazoned and while the impact now is negligible, it was disastrous then. With that confrontation, with the searing white-hot words, we separated. We never discussed the incident again, never resolved it, the distance between us immeasurable. My resentment and bewilderment grew. I remember the pain.

Southern women are raised to be husband-pleasers. Pleasing him should not be this difficult.

Incompatibility – I considered it grounds for divorce. Two children. Church. Friends. Marriage vows. How juvenile I felt when I balanced the strengths in our marriage. My spirit was crushed and my heart broken as I contemplated my shortcomings listed for me by my husband.

While I had not been "unhappy," now I was profoundly sad; a deep penetrating sadness covered me as I feigned that everything's fine. Life. Day in and day out. Smile. Too much was at stake to be petty.

Consumed with worry for our future and burdened with being someone who did not meet my husband's expectations of a wife, I was someone who caused irritation and displeasure. I determined to change. If I were different, he'd love me. He loved me once, I believed. I could recapture the good if something changed. And that would be me.

I decided somehow to become a better version of myself. How had I changed into a demanding shrew? Perhaps I'd always been one. I contemplated my options.

Southern women are raised to be husband-pleasers. Pleasing him should not be so difficult. A communication specialist taught me techniques to open lines of communication, such as how to use "I statements." I embraced a less demanding demeanor and stated how I felt. Plain and simple. I desired peace within my life and would do anything within my power to improve our marriage.

Husband and Wife. Two children plus a dog and a goldfish. Church. Family and Friends. Careers. The American Dream on a beautiful Christmas card.

Day in. Day out. "Is he?"

Ups and Downs. "Could he be …?"

Laughter and Tears. "What if he's…?"

A kiss at midnight on New Year's Eve. "Surely he's not having an affair."

I'll change.

Let me count the ways I love… the dream.

Chapter 4 – Let Me Count the Ways - Reflection:

Read the following scripture. Next, write a personal reflection about the meaning of each scripture for your life.

Matthew 11: 28-30 – *"Come unto me, all ye that labour and are heavy laden, and I will give you rest. Take my yoke upon you, and learn of me; for I am meek and lowly in heart: and ye shall find rest unto your souls. For my yoke is easy, and my burden is light."*

Luke 12:25-27 – *"And which of you with taking thought can add to his stature one cubit? If ye then be not able to do that thing which is least, why take you thought for the rest? Consider the lilies how they grow; they toil not, they spin not; and yet I say unto you, that Solomon in all his glory was not arrayed like one of these."*

Tart Lesson: Listen first.　　　　　　　　　　*Sweet Pleasure: God is speaking.*

Chapter 4 – Let Me Count the Ways - Food for Thought:

Comfort food. In a cookie tin was a cache of warm, salted pecans. With my grandmother in the back seat and my parents in the front, the heater blowing full blast, we motored to a traditional football rivalry. The best part of the trip was convincing grandmother to open the pecan tin.

She and all the grown-up ladies roasted and salted these pecans during the fall, as her home place was covered with pecan trees. Picking up the pecans, cracking them, shelling, picking out, and then freezing them until ready for a multitude of uses was a family event. We'd make candy with family recipes including divinity and fondant ovals with pecan halves on each side. At Christmas, we'd color the fondant pink and light green.

At the center of childhood memories are the canopies formed by pecan trees. Their shelter was comforting, as was the memory of salted pecans.

Salted Pecans (Supply of pecans is plentiful and just about any chocolate recipe can be improved with ½ cup of pecan pieces.)

Melt 1 stick of putter and pour over one pound of pecan halves in a shallow pan. Bake for 1 hour at 275 degrees, stirring occasionally. Drain on paper towels.
Salt well. Add a generous sprinkling of sugar, also.
Cooked nuts should be stored in air-tight container.

CHAPTER 5

Going to the Mattresses: Fight for Survival

Sitting undressed in an unfashionable, tacky sheet upon the examination table at the gynecologist is cold and nerve-wracking. I was somewhat calmed when the doctor and his nurse came into the room and assured me that "it's probably nothing" because I had always been faithful and regular in my check-ups.

But, when I lay back and he looked at and pressed on my abdomen, his face paled. I was quickly scheduled for an ultrasound. I could not see what the nurse was viewing but her manner suggested trouble. After the test in the back rooms of the clinic, I was tenderly escorted into my doctor's private office where I waited, not knowing what to expect. My mind was open but blank – devoid of fear, also devoid of thought. What day is this?

The weekend:

The school year events had come to a confetti-festive conclusion and teachers were gathering their belongings and planning for a summer of travel or summer conferences, yard work or continuing education. Every day was a challenge, a hurdle, a monument to teenage angst. With a deep sigh and dreams of solitary bubble-baths, I drove slowly home from the commencement ceremony. Reflecting on the year, I had survived a monstrous learning curve and vowed to move forward. The clouds were parting.

The weekend had been a busy one, and one filled with relief at the prospect of a summer with a different pace. I took my time preparing for bed that Sunday evening, knowing that the alarm would not wake me at 5:30 AM.

I stepped from the bathtub after a luxurious bubble bath and walked over to the closet, passing the mirror and glancing at my mid-life body. I was smiling to myself, remembering an old joke, and pressing on my slightly *poochy* tummy, like the panel of a modest form-shaper. I nearly fainted at what I felt.

Though I had not gained any weight, I had begun to outgrow the midsection of my skirts. So, with the thought, "This is ridiculous," and with a turn to the mirror and pressure to my abdomen, alas, I nearly collapsed when I felt something. White-hot fear shot through me; I felt light headed, faint, and clammy cold. While I knew nothing of what it might be, I knew with certainty, something was not normal.

That night, with my husband out of town at a conference and the kids asleep, as I lay still in bed, I applied pressure to the suspect area, willing "it" to evaporate, disappear, vaporize, be an imaginary blip on the radar screen. However, when I awakened the next morning, the blinding fear was still with me.

I went to work, finishing out the paperwork for the school year and preparing for summer school formalities. At work, I telephoned my doctor. His nurse said, "Oh, I'm certain it's nothing, but if it'll make you feel calmer, less upset, come in around 1 PM."

You bet I am coming in.

And, here I am sitting in an oversized, brown leather chair in the office of my gynecologist. Something is majorly wrong.

My gynecologist entered the room and sat in front of me, not behind his desk. Recall if you can Lily Tomlin's role in the movie *The Incredible Shrinking Woman*. If you know the movie, then you recall the image of a woman experiencing "shrinkage." As the doctor talked to me, I heard the teacher voice from *Peanuts' Charlie Brown and*

Snoopy Cartoons: *"WaaWaaWaaWaaWaa."* I wrote the words "complete hysterectomy," "CA-125, blood test," and "granular, some fluid filled" and then "strange word with -onoma as a suffix." I was told I would know more when the blood test results came in the next week, but the news did not seem good. I was withering, sinking into the brown leather chair in his office. My vision became fuzzy; my hearing was distorted by the ringing in my ears. What I was trying to comprehend would change my life forever, and the lives of my family and friends.

He asked me if I wanted to call anyone to come get me, to drive. I shook my head "no." My husband was out of town, my parents were keeping my younger son and the older son was at home with friends. No, I'll be fine. I drove to my parents' home and told them in as matter-of-fact manner as possible that I was to have surgery, a complete hysterectomy. "Why? What's wrong?"

Even then, I did not admit the obvious. "There is a mass and it might be malignant. But, don't worry, they'll get it out and I'll be fine." That was a rather simplistic report and one that was not quite accurate, but it was all I could formulate into words.

When I left their condominium, holding it all together for the sake of everyone else, my mother fell apart and went further down the rabbit's hole as the night progressed. She was taken by ambulance to the local hospital, experiencing her first bout with congestive heart failure. Pity my father. His wife was in one hospital on a respirator, and his daughter had just been diagnosed with cancer.

Within the next few hours my husband returned home from his conference and I told him of the ordeal that Monday afternoon. I also told him about the blood tests and upcoming x-rays and CT scans.

While at work the next week, I received the call from my gynecologist telling me that the blood test CA-125 reported the highest number they had ever observed, an absolute certainty for advanced ovarian cancer. He would schedule my surgery immediately and put me in touch with an oncologist. My husband already had made an appointment for me with the most noted oncologist in the area, a marvelously sensitive and superbly competent oncologist, trained at Memorial Sloan-Kettering.

I lost my innocence when I heard the words ovarian cancer. I knew nothing of Gilda Radner's struggle except for her character's struggle to make Chevy Chase understand her position on very important issues as Roseann-Roseannadanna on SNL. "Never Mind" that I had no comprehension of the road I would travel, nor did I fully grasp the horrific seriousness of what presented itself in my life. I did feel that I would be losing everything within me that was associated with femininity, with being a woman. I would lose those things, but perhaps I would not lose my life.

After incredibly high numbers on the CA-125 test and other conclusive tests and results pinpointing Stage "right at 4" and complexity, a complete hysterectomy was ordered and scheduled along with additional CT scan, a MRI, and X-rays. The life of a believed-to-be completely healthy 44-year-old woman with one child a rising 9th grader and another child who just turned 4 years old was changed beyond recognition. I became too quickly a woman owning a life-threatening disease that had come upon me with no recognizable warning.

Vaguely I recalled a precautionary statement through customary dialogue over fifteen years previous. Cancer can occur in women who take fertility drugs, in women who bear no children. After years of trying to conceive, we had adopted two infants, the last child mid-way through my 40th year. I had become a player in a statistical game of chance. I had given the *Wheel* a final spin and hit bankrupt. The pea was not under my shell. Snake-eyes had turned up and the player went bust.

My friends met together for prayer and determined a plan to support me and my children.

The same scenario took place within my church. I was held securely in the hands of loving friends. My husband's focus was singular. Friends reported to me that he was clearly devoted to me and to my recovery.

Alfred, Lord Tennyson's Ulysses: "To strive, to seek, to find, and not to yield."

That June I underwent radical abdominal surgery in which everything possibly affected by the cancer was removed. I saw interns whose youthful appearance caused friends to tag them with nicknames such as Doogie Howser. I would go to sleep praying and wake up praying.

I vaguely recall the television scenes and the nurses' discussion of OJ Simpson's van on the Los Angeles freeway in June, 1994, but I was one who could honestly say I was unaffected by Nicole Simpson's murder, except symbolically.

My own life, I felt, had been stolen; in a bizarre way, I had been slashed and the life I had envisioned was taken. Something vague and protective overtook me as I determined what course I would take. Remaining stoic and resolute seemed the best management technique.

I chose to remain sheltered from the full implication of the diagnosis. It was far too bleak a picture, too fatalistic an attitude for me to comprehend. My husband was beside me through all those early years of the battle and behaved as a devoted husband and father. I put on blinders and plowed forward into ground for which I had only one plan – survival.

In the movie *You've Got Mail*, Meg Ryan's character is confiding to Tom Hanks' character about the struggle she is experiencing with the possible closing of her family's bookstore. Tom Hanks' character replies that she must go to the mattresses, a line from the movie, *The Godfather*. Whatever it takes, pull out the big dogs, and wrestle the devil if necessary. She must hold nothing back. She must fight for herself and for what she wants. Sometimes, you have to fight for your very life.

During the six years of treatment, I struggled through multiple recurrences, years of monthly and/or weekly chemotherapy, and medicine cabinets stuffed with samples of anti-nausea drugs, none of which worked. I could walk into the clinic and become violently ill. I prayed to live long enough for my four-year-old to become more independent.

I also prayed that the chemo could be administered in such a routine manner so that I could remain the hub of my home, for my children to enjoy a relatively normal life. My husband had a new focus- keeping my treatment schedule and our finances in order.

I was hoping to receive treatments as a diabetic receives insulin injections. What I did not comprehend was that chemotherapy is a poison; it kills and destroys. How innocently ignorant I was about it all. Insulin is life-saving for those who require it. The dosage in cancer treatment must be carefully measured so that it will not kill the patient. In its pharmacology, it will target and destroy every cancer cell even though it also kills multitudes of good cells, too. A person cannot survive with poison pumped continuously through the blood, month after month and year after year. Surviving chemotherapy is as important as surviving the disease itself.

Chapter 5 – Going to the Mattresses: Fight for Survival - Reflection:

The event in your life that impacted you the most probably was not cancer. That is wonderful. But, to date, there has been some event that you had to dig deep to face. Name it and thank God for leading your path through it.

Read the following scripture. Next, write a personal reflection about the meaning of each scripture for your life.

Psalm 37: 5-6 – *"Commit thy way unto the Lord; trust also in him; and he shall bring it to pass. And he shall bring forth thy righteousness as the light, and thy judgment as the noonday."*

Deuteronomy 31: 8 – *"And the Lord, he it is that doth go before thee; he will be with thee, he will not fail thee, neither forsake thee: fear not, neither be dismayed."*

Proverbs 3: 5-6 – *"Trust in the Lord with all thine heart; and lean not unto thine own understanding. In all thy ways acknowledge him, and he shall direct thy paths."*

Tart Lesson: Cancer can hit any family.   *Sweet Pleasure: Family & friend show love.*

Chapter 5 – Going to the Mattresses: Fight for Survival - Food for Thought:

Google (verb) "recipes.com" or "recipes cancer patients" and you'll be inundated with links.

We cook to show concern, to heal, to celebrate. We prepare meals to display our love, our compassion, and to say "this is your favorite and it's just for you." The presentation of the meal has become critical as to how it's received – just the right texture, color combinations, and a variety of nutrients are important to a wonderful meal, and to cancer patients who taste and smell differently during chemotherapy. Whether "just for two" or a tableful of diners, a well-planned and prepared meal soothes those who enjoy the meal.

When I was battling cancer, dishes tasted metallic if I used a silver-plated fork and were bland if not spiced with plenty of salt, pepper, and onion. I drank V-8 juice often and to the glass rim I added a margarita-like salt ring. I broke out in red whelps from that overage. Keeping calorie intake high is important for the battle.

I use *Penzey's Spices* for meats, desserts, and vegetables. Their shop and online catalog carry many of my secret ingredients. It is with pleasure that I add Mexican vanilla, Pork Chop seasoning, Chicago Steak seasoning, Lemon zest, and Vietnamese cinnamon to my favorite creations.

Broccoli Cheese Soup -This recipe may be made spicier with more pepper. While being treated with chemotherapy, food that is bland takes on the taste of the container in which it was prepared – aluminum or metal or such. Plastic utensils should be used because even forks taste bad! Hot, spicy foods and juices (like V-8 with added salt!) taste better than anything.

3 cans Cream of Mushroom soup   3cups milk
1 roll/brick garlic cheese   2 pkgs frozen chopped broccoli

Mix soup and milk and cheese and let simmer while broccoli cooks, according to the package.
Add to the mixture and mix well.
S & P to taste.

CHAPTER 6

Goodbye, Bikini Hello, Ann-Margret

"Yes, you'll lose your hair. Maybe not all of it, but most.

No, it won't drop out, or fall out onto your pillow. As you comb, brush it, or shampoo it, the hair will be in the drain or on the towel.

Don't be alarmed, but the hair loss will include eyebrows, eyelashes, all body hair.

You'll need a wig."

They recommended a local shop meeting needs of women with cancer.

I was nervous about the appointment, and the shop owner did not know specifically what I was there to choose, or why.

I had made a private appointment, the only kind they make, for protection of the individual going through the trauma. My friend and I walked in and were greeted graciously by the kindest lady, "Oh, Sweetie," she said, "you're gonna' be just fine. We're going to fix you right up. No one will ever know you've had a mastectomy."

How sad is that. I had lost enough weight in the early stages of surgery and treatment that she thought I'd had a mastectomy. She would have sold me boobs. Maybe it's BOGO! I never had a movie star bust line, but, I did not think *the girls* were non-existent! Regardless of the faux-pas, I laughed at the mistake. "Perhaps," I said, "we could take some butt cheeks and add the bulk to the top half of my body."

I chose a glamorous wig in about the same reddish brown color of my hair. I was wearing my hair longer, so I decided to go with the *Ann-Margret* look, hoping to summons Elvis for a magical trip to Las Vegas, somewhere other than here. Though I named her Mildred ("Hold on to Mildred. That wind off the river will send her flying."), the natural-hair wig was anything but old-school.

Experiencing the loss of my (any woman's) crowning glory offered a great deal of opportunity for humility. Gaining humility, understanding that life comes to everyone in the same manner, sparing no one from all its elements, is one of the greatest gifts I received. In addition to humility, I gained a much softer heart and surer belief in the vitality of the human spirit that sustains us. The old wineskin was lost and what was found was a new and improved model – a woman with more compassion and sensitivity. What I lost was replaced by what God alone can supply. And, I gained pounds-a-plenty.

I took prescription drugs (steroids) to decrease nausea and improve my sense of well-being. The side-effects included increased appetite. As a result, I ate everything in sight. Driving home from work, I was often allured by the aroma of barbecue or fresh baked cookies, cakes and dozens of donuts. I would detour and devour a sandwich or a dessert, driving around neighborhoods, gobbling grub like a starved dog. My cravings were never actually satisfied by the amount of food intake, but my ability to withstand rounds of chemotherapy improved.

In losing my stomach muscles I lost my bikini figure, because the incision is vertical rather than horizontal, thus cutting through the muscles. As a bonus, I gained cleavage over the course of the chemotherapy. The doctors were happy I was gaining weight rather than losing it. Perhaps finally having cleavage is not such a bad trade off. Anything seasoned with excessive amounts of sugar, salt, onions, and spices tasted delicious and I ate to dull the bad taste in my mouth, but never really enjoyed the food. Everything bland tasted of aluminum or worse.

Sunrise in a Lemon Sky

I wanted my life and a future. Therefore, I fought hard. I used all kinds of weapons including food, diversion, work, play, and above all else, prayer.

Believing in the healing power of God, I pursued my treatment like a woman possessed. I continued to work, continued to be a mom and a wife. I went to work after chemotherapy treatments. I climbed the stairs, pulling my body up, step by step. I would not give in or give up; I would not sit at home and ponder my situation. Instead, I stuffed my brain and conscious thought with work, details of anything that contained facts and figures. I was unable to read a magazine or a novel but I wanted no quiet time unless I was asleep. My brain could not handle the quiet; I filled it with anything not related to cancer.

Former cancer patients or those still in the treatment protocol called me out of a desire to help. One lady asked me pointed questions and to each I answered, "I don't know." She became exasperated with me and said in disgusted exasperation, "You are so naïve." Perhaps that was my plan, to remain so naïve that I totally believed I would not die. I never took another call from that good intentioned lady. Other people called, out of curiosity more than anything else. I gave them nothing but positive comments. It was my BFFs who knew the truth.

> *Friends stepped in and guarded me from drowning in reality. These precious friends refused to give up on me and helped me in my diversions – do anything, say anything, just get through this horror.*

These were the friends who knew they did not have to say anything. They were present. These perfect friends sustained me and my children. They kept vigil at the hospital. They stayed with me while I slept, stayed with my children. They were there when I woke up. Where was he? He was at work or at a church meeting or at choir practice or somewhere.

Friends stepped in and guarded me from drowning in reality. These precious friends refused to give up on me and helped me in my diversions – do anything, say anything, just get through this horror.

Had I read the medical reports on my cancer, had I delved into Internet searches, I would have been inundated with a bleak prognosis. Some say we each must own our cancer and be involved in our treatment programs. I was totally involved, but in a different way. For me, I turned all the nasty details over to God, my surgeon, and my oncologist. This disease was something I had not the tiniest bit of control over. I could, however, control my attitude, my dogged perseverance, and my daily routine. I was living *when bad things happen to good people* in front of my children, and I refused to be a weak sister.

Relegating the cancer to a corner of my life became my method of dealing with the treatment regimen. Diversion became important also in my recovery plan. Walking into a treatment center provoked tears and vomit, before the first IV went in. Nights seemed endless and on some days, on the floor in the bathroom, death felt imminent. God held my hand. He said, "Everything will be all right." And I knew it would be, but had to realize that with God, everything *is* all right.

When it was time for treatments, I got into the *treatment box*. While there, I endured. When it was over, I got out of the box and lived as close to a normal life as possible. My husband managed the finances and record keeping with the insurance companies. During the first years, and certainly the first months of the diagnosis and protocol, he fully supported me in my battle. Through it all, he remained physically present; he was there.

These chemotherapy sessions had become familiar in their routine and the nurses knew that I needed fluids and anti-nausea drugs during the infusion hours. Regardless of the precautions, the result was nausea and vomiting, as I transported the hanging bags with me to the restroom. Ultimately, the nurses gave me *happy drugs* the moment I arrived at the clinic. The drug I recall most clearly is Ativan. It calmed me sufficiently and reduced my anxiety to allow a successful treatment.

During the time of the chemotherapy treatments, stories could not hold my concentration. My mind would not focus sufficiently and would drift into scenarios that were too preoccupied with cancer and survival. To combat that situation, I worked. I could concentrate on details, facts, numbers, and concrete evidence, writing reports, adding comments, verifying statistics, and completing paperwork. The next week, recovered from the treatment and returned to work, I would read the reports and marvel at the excellent work someone had completed. I did not remember writing a single word, but recognized my phrasing and documentation. It was a remarkable experience.

> *What does cancer have to do with marriage? At the beginning, it was glue: warriors against a common enemy.*

While I believe that God's healing can come even if we experience a physical death, I also believe that God intervenes. I read the book *Cancervive* (sic) and it was hugely inspirational for me. In addition, the book entitled *Hope and Healing* published by the Church Health Center provided encouragement. It contains a collection of sermons about both Hope and Healing, written by some of the most influential pastors in the area, regardless of denomination. I prayed without ceasing, went to sleep praying and woke up praying. What I prayed for was survival and healing. Prayer groups, led by friends in various congregations, prayed for the same thing.

The most remarkable experience I had out of those prayers was the certain assurance that God would not leave me and would "hold me in the palm of His hand." I believe that God gave me a vision of Him doing exactly that and I heard God speak those words of assurance to me. "I will never leave you or forsake you. I hold you in the palm of my hand." The vision was of God's hands open, palms up and I was within His hands. I never doubted God. I never believed for a moment that I would die.

During the early days of the diagnosis, my older son cut straight to the heart of the matter. After I told him of my diagnosis, he asked me. "Are you going to die?"

I told him, "No."

He walked away and said, "Ok, then. You'll be alright. It'll be ok."

That's the way he and I handled it. He and I each behaved as if nothing was out of the ordinary. He acknowledged my illness and was kind and thoughtful when I was vomiting my guts out in my bathroom, asking, "Can I get you anything, Mom." He did not disturb me when I was sleeping for days. He did not act out in disrespect or in any attention-seeking manner.

The younger son knew nothing different. He was only four years old, so he was raised with his mother being sick. We made sure his life was as joyous as any four year old. My parents and husband supported them through their childhoods. None of us belabored the reality of cancer and how it impacted life as we knew it. We cried privately.

I endured years of chemotherapy because of multiple recurrences. Some people believed I would die and at one particularly low point, had about a year to live. I was not told that information because I was in such a good frame of mind to fight the disease. The reason all my family joined together one Christmas with my parents was because my ex-husband had told them that it would be my last Christmas. He had been told that I could not endure the chemotherapy much longer and that within a year, I would require hospice care.

One thing I am grateful to him for is this: he refused to let negative people or negative messages around me. I never knew that grim prognosis. It's a good thing I did not know what others thought. I am glad they did not tell me, because I fought constantly, like a woman possessed of but one goal: survival for my family and for my children.

So, what does cancer have to do with marriage? At the beginning, it was glue: warriors against a common enemy. But, as treatments continued and living with cancer became more of a sickening reality, my ex-husband began, I believe, to make plans for living without me, one way or another.

Chapter 6 – Goodbye, Bikini – Hello, Ann-Margret - Reflection:

Has there ever been a time in your life when outside, uncontrollable events damaged you in any way? How did you respond? Write about taking the whole problem to God.

God can heal a person in a variety of ways. There is spiritual healing, emotional healing, as well as physical healing. God heals us daily. Write about what you consider God's healing to be for you and your life, for your loved ones.

While I do wish I could have become the person I am today without it, my great aunt wrote to me that the cancer has a way of refining a person and that this and other troubles are used by God to hone a person into a better version of themselves. What is your understanding in this regard?

Read the following scripture. Next, write a personal reflection about the meaning of each scripture for your life.

2 Corinthians 1: 3-4 – *"Blessed be God, even the Father of our Lord Jesus Christ, the Father of mercies, and the God of comfort; Who comforteth us in all our tribulation, that we may be able to comfort them which are in any trouble, by the comfort wherewith we ourselves are comforted of God."*

Tart Lesson: Battling cancer is horrid.   *Sweet Pleasure: Compassion and sensitivity emerge.*

Chapter 6 – Good-bye, Bikini – Hello, Ann-Margret - Food for Thought:

My mother was a great cook, but she did not like cooking. In my earliest years as we lived with my grandmother, it was Mamie whose presence ruled the kitchen. Mother made a marvelous roast, potatoes and carrots in our later childhood. Maybe it was Mamie's recipe that she served along with another of Mamie's creations: those tiny, delicious *little biscuits* for Sunday dinner. I recall that Mamie allowed me to don an apron and bake a "salt cake" and take it to Daddy for him and his salesman to enjoy. Imagine their faces as they watched me anticipate my daddy's delightful but puckered expression, "delicious, Honey." White granular substances are as difficult to differentiate as are lettuce and cabbage when there is no skill. Mother was far too impatient to tolerate a little girl in the kitchen. She prepared our morning and evening meals, and scowled if anyone showed up for lunch.

Usually, cooks limit "salt" in their recipes. However, with patients who crave spice and anything that is not bland, I'd recommend this recipe. Do, however, watch the salt intake!

KICKIN' CHICKIN' VEGETABLE SOUP:

1 can each:

chicken broth	chopped tomato bits
V-8 juice (secret ingredient!)	tomato, onion, peppers

Add

shoepeg corn	sliced carrots
cut green beans	sliced potatoes
tiny baby peas	chicken pieces, seasoned

Heat thoroughly and allow to simmer for several hours to absorb flavors. Use salt, pepper, and Cavender's Seasoning and Penzey's Spices- choice. The spicier the soup, the better it will taste.

Chapter 7

You Can-Survive

"What's wrong?" She'd heard me sniffle and glanced over her shoulder.

Head bowed, I'm silent, except for a muffled sob.

"You're crying." She began to pull to the side of the road.

They started handing me tissues.

Once discovered, I let it out and sobbed, having begun to cry with a single tear escaping, and then another, and another.

"Ok, what's going on? Tell us right now." She put on the brake and shifted into Park. "Are you hurting?"

Slobbering and blubbering, I confessed: "I don't want to go home. I can't do this any more."

I was referring to coping with reality. We were driving closer and closer to months of additional chemotherapy which meant vomiting, hair-loss, wigs, fatigue, and more vomiting. Also, I knew that I would be going back into a home where the reality was bleak and one I did not want to face. I dreaded keeping up the front, even for my dear sons.

We all cried.

At an earlier time in this ordeal: Because of highly advanced and aggressive professional treatment with phenomenal oncologists at a well-known cancer clinic, because they are Godly people and are involved with their patients, providing treatment on a personal basis, I had weathered treatments and was healing and surviving. God helped me fight and gave illumination to my plight, hearing and answering prayers continuously brought to His throne.

God's hand is always involved with medical miracles, but at that time I was in a tremendous fight for my very life. Steroid dose packs, constant inflow of anti-nausea drugs through a portable pump, weekly chemotherapy, deep fatigue and hair loss, I was immersed in whatever came next to prolong my life.

Because of constant prayer, prayers from groups and individuals everywhere, prayer at every moment throughout every day, I was surviving. I did not ever quit fighting for my life.

Disease happens regardless of personal faith and walk with God. What the person does after the diagnosis is what magnifies the walk with God.

Just when the check-ups were extending from monthly to every three months and I'd relax just a bit, there would be a recurrence. We'd fight the disease anew and add new drugs to the chemotherapy protocol. Another successful treatment regimen would extend the check-ups from three months to four months to six. I would start to believe that this nightmare might end. It would begin again with the discovery of another spot on my colon, but the cancer cells were still ovarian. This routine was becoming demoralizing and my attitude was becoming fatalistic.

That day, I sat in the examination room as the radiologist read the CT films. I waited and seconds ticked in my brain. My ears strained for sounds from the hallway. Then, the door opened and he had no smile.

"It's back. Come with me," he said. I stood in front of my films, noting the tiny spot on my colon that was going to kill me if something different did not happen. The oncologists had said we could not continue chemotherapy with constant recurrences. The poison would kill me before the cancer. The body cannot withstand that kind of battering. Only one route seemed feasible: a rare second surgery, if the surgeon agreed.

In my case, the ovarian cancer had recurred in only one spot on my colon. It recurred in the same spot each time, and was amazingly not evidenced anywhere else, so they said let's get rid of this thing, and hope for the best. Pray for the best is more like it.

In cancers such as mine, second surgeries are not performed routinely because in recurrences, chemotherapy has not done the trick in totality; the cancer is probably elsewhere. In my case, miraculously, that was not the case. I was a candidate for a second surgery.

Prior to the morning surgery, lying in a drugged state on the rolling bed that delivers patients to the surgical table, my surgeon appeared. Her nurse was at my side, also. I grabbed their hands, and through tears, I begged them to get this done and get it all. There is no need to do a so-called exploratory look. We know it's there; we know it's malignant. Just do it. "Get it out of me," I recall pleading, tears flooding my eyes. My surgeon said, "Let's get this done." And then, the nurse pushed the rest of the drugs into my veins and I was asleep, still praying, I am sure.

The surgery and the months of chemotherapy that followed proved successful. I am one of God's miracles.

To celebrate that surgical success that led to ultimate success, prior to the chemotherapy sessions that eradicated any remaining cellular grains, my girlfriends and I planned a trip. I needed a reprieve, moments of celebration and fun. These friends did everything they knew to cheer me, to sustain me, to help me and my children. We rented a condo and borrowed a wheelchair. It was rather funny the way we traveled, and we had a wonderful time. They pampered me, as only girl friends can do.

My parents were at my house and so was my husband, with Mother and Daddy looking after the children. I was so grateful to my parents, and to him, for allowing time for me in this manner. But, not one time did that man call me during the trip. Not one time did he check on my health, my stamina.

He gave me a puppy. In retrospect, it was a terrific trade.

The confession that I did not want to go home occurred as this brief escape was coming to an end.

I did go home, of course, and I did undergo the next drug regimen.

I continued to parent and work to the very best of my ability. I trudged through, head high in public. At one point, my husband told me, "I admire you." I wanted his love, that deep assurance of knitted souls; admiration seemed condescending, and I told him so. I wanted to slap him into my reality.

About ten months later, tests revealed that the ovarian cancer cells removed in the colon resection had not regrown. They had died a thousand deaths and nothing was visible nor was there a bad blood report. Life was looking good. In fact, my husband told me when we left the treatment center with a wonderful outlook and a miraculous report of *all clear*, it was the happiest day of his life.

I thought it was because we could start our life again with good health all around, an answered prayer. I was wrong.

Now, without my knowledge, he began syphoning money from our joint checking account and depositing it into an account of his own. Had I died, he could have become a widower. For my spouse, it would have been easier had I died because he would have been a martyr, set free with no questions asked.

A protocol is available for surviving cancer today. No drugs can rescue a marriage. That winter, he gave me a puppy and never slept in our bed again. In retrospect, it was a terrific trade.

Even though I follow Alfred, Lord Tennyson's **Ulysses** in philosophy, "To strive, to seek, to find, and not to yield" in just about everything, I did have to acknowledge that I had reached a point where I could do nothing. Now there were two single adults living together, destroying the very ideal love that God had envisioned for his children. One person alone cannot save a marriage, or destroy it, for that matter. As they say, it takes two.

We survived cancer, but could we survive marriage?

Chapter 7 – Can-Survive - Reflection:

Read the following scripture. Next, write a personal reflection about the meaning of each scripture for your life.

Philippians 3: 13 – *"Bretheren, I count not myself to have apprehended: but this one thing I do, forgetting those things which are behind, and reaching forth unto those things which are before."*

Philippians 4:13: *"I can do all things through Christ which strengtheneth me."*

Tart Lesson: Chemotherapy is Ugly.   Sweet Pleasure: Friends are Beautiful.

Chapter 7 – Can-Survive - Food for Thought:

Who can top the scene in *Fried Green Tomatoes at the Whistle Stop Café* when the body of Ruth's abusive husband, Frank, is disposed of in a barbecue pit and served with a special sauce? The Whistle Stop Café serves nothing but the best in barbecue, especially to obnoxious law enforcement officers.

DEATH BY CHOCOLATE
Make your best and gooiest Brownie recipe and prick holes.

Measure 1/4 cup Kahlua (or flavoring) and pour it into pricked holes you've made in the Brownies.

Prepare according to package directions:
    1 pkg JELLO Chocolate Mousse.
    Open a container of Cool Whip (8 oz)
    Chop up pecans (1/2 cup of chopped nuts)

Crush 3 Heath bars.
Alternately layer the Brownies, Mousse, Cool Whip, Pecans and Heath Bars Finish off with dollops of Cool Whip and Crushed Heath Bar.

CHAPTER 8

Chainsaw Massacre

I thought my husband was lying. I knew he was staying in another bedroom from time to time, experimenting with questionable web sites, and staying away from home as much as possible. I'd read of a man's mid-life crisis, even "manopause." He was in a crisis, I was sure.

I never summoned enough gumption to call his hand on the behaviors, but expressed concern for the misery he obviously felt. Wrapped up in a troubled marriage I wanted to save and in a family worth every insulting, demeaning behavior I could endure, I thought our troubles were my fault, either for being sick or for losing my edge as a woman.

"You seem very troubled. Why not go to a counselor. I'd go, too. It might help you, and us."

He did not. We did not. Not then, not ever.

So, life played out.

Unprepared for what happened in March, 2000, perhaps as blindsided as the United States would be on September 11, 2001, I listened when he said these words:

"I have an apartment."

"What did you say?"

"I have an apartment. I am moving out."

Rewind: The afternoon was Friday. We had met with a financial planner to obtain a loan to pay debt that I believed we jointly had accumulated during the years of fighting cancer. He said he was taking the loan himself, but I needed to be there since we were a married couple. Sitting at the table with the loan papers in front of me giving answers about our marital status, I focused on one statement: we are married.

Our relationship had been so strained that I was hoping his answers revealed that he wanted an improved marital relationship with me, as I had begged him several months prior to seek either medical attention or help from a psychologist. I did not know, nor did I want to know, what a pawn I was.

Friday evening, after the meeting with the financial operatives that afternoon, I went out to dinner. It had been a year, and I was declared *cancer free*, and this Spring Break, unlike the previous one, was going to be different – no chemotherapy, no wigs, no cancer. We went over to a girl friend's house for dessert. Several of us were celebrating the beginning of some breathing room from our jobs. We were light-hearted and having a wonderful time with stories and jokes and plans for tomorrow. On the drive home, I was as unaware as I could possibly be for what lay in wait behind the door I would soon open, declaring, "Hey, you guys. I'm home."

I walked into the den and the three of us- father, mother, and child -visited for a while about friends, the dinner, and what my men had done for fun while I was with the girls. I went on to the bedroom to get ready for bed. Friday nights were routinely very relaxing and I was looking forward to a warm bath, my nightclothes, sleeping late on Saturday, and a wonderful week of total relaxation. The older son was away at college and the younger son was also beginning his Spring Break. Nothing, absolutely nothing showed up on the radar for the bomb that was about to explode in my face.

My husband walked into the bedroom, casually over to his side of the bed, sat down, propped up, and lay back on the pillows. I was in bed, also propped up, about to turn on the television and pull out some new fashion magazines. I knew that trouble existed in the marriage, which by now was closer to an inferno than any part of paradise, but with every tiny nuance of normalcy, I gained some degree of hope.

When I look back at the excuses I made for each insulting behavior, I wonder how much self-esteem I actually possessed at that time. When I look back, I wonder why I wanted the marriage to be saved; the only reason worth thinking about was "for the children." The marriage we shared was one of obligation and duty. We'd been through so much.

That evening, from the lines of a rehearsed speech, he began with reminding me how I had begged him to see a counselor. Further, he reminded me that we had both become miserable in the marriage. The difference between us was that I believed it was a phase, a cycle that all marriages must endure in order to survive. He saw it differently. So, while I thought that this conversation was headed in a positive direction, he uttered a statement I thought I would never hear, not ever in my life.

"I have an apartment."

With that statement, my life, our family changed. Everything dissolved before me. My head spun, my heart raced, my ears rang, and my vision blurred. It was similar to the shrinking I experienced in the brown leather chair in my gynecologist's office six years before. Since I existed with humiliation anyway, what was one more dagger if it could save our family.

> *It seems he had taken out a loan and then proceeded to take me to the cleaners.*

I begged him to stay, to reconsider, change his mind. Nothing I could do or say would keep him from moving out the next morning.

I asked him if there was someone else. I had believed that possibility years earlier but flowers had convinced me otherwise. He said, "No. I just do not want to be married with a wife, two kids, and a dog in the suburbs any longer." No more American Dream Christmas cards for us. Seems he had stayed through the cancer. That was behind us now. I had hoped for a new beginning. He had already planned for one.

He moved out.

It seems he had taken out a loan and then proceeded to take me to the cleaners.

He left the marriage, the mortgage, a leaking hot water heater, an overgrown back yard, crumbling shutters, all the past-due bills, and a depleted bank account. The new reality he professed was that "he gave me everything."

Yes, he gave me the whole mess he had created.

Too long in denial, I struggled and delayed over a year from this point, actually on my birthday, before I filed for divorce. It took that entire year before I gave up the senseless struggle and I filed for divorce. The painful legal and spiritual process of tearing apart a thirty-year marriage leaves deep wounds and gaping holes where hope, trust, and love had been.

When two people become one flesh, there is no clean, surgical incision that can separate the two people involved. When the covenant of marriage is broken, when intimacy is lost, none of the individuals will ever breathe in quite the same way.

Ignorance had woven an invisible thread through the tapestry of our marriage; betrayal snagged it. The whole piece came apart at the seams. Weakened and flawed much earlier, the tapestry held together by habit. The day of awareness had yet to dawn.

Chapter 8 – Chainsaw Massacre - Reflection:

List all the things you think you could have said or done that would have made any difference in your past relationship(s).

If you think that saying or doing anything differently would make you feel better about your break-up, do you have opportunity to do so?

Are you willing to work hard at your marriage for a year? You'd then know you tried everything. After that, turn him over to God.

Read the following scripture. Next, write a personal reflection about the meaning of each scripture for your life.

Psalm 25: 1-2, 4 - *"Unto thee, O Lord, do I lift up my soul. O my God, I trust in thee; let me not be ashamed, let not mine enemies triumph over me. Shew me thy ways, O Lord; teach me they paths."*

Tart Lesson: Marriages can end.   *Sweet Pleasure: Denial can end, also.*

Chapter 8 – Chainsaw Massacre - Food for Thought:

My ex-husband believed that he could cook, so he followed a recipe for a Florentine quiche. It was nasty, salty, bitter, disgusting. It tasted beyond bad. How could a person mess up a quiche? He might as well make a mess of green bean casserole which is incredibly difficult to do. I dumped the remains into a brown paper bag and put it all into the garbage. He retrieved it and fertilized the back yard tomato plants with the concoction. They died.

Flower Pot Dessert
(Worms in Dirt)
   Recipe: Buy a nice size plastic flower pot. Line it with aluminum foil first and then cling-wrap.

3oz. pkg. Cream Cheese	1 stick butter (margarine)
Vanilla Instant Pudding Mix (2pkgs)	3½ cups Milk
	1 pkg Oreo Cookies
12 oz. carton Cool Whip	

Prepare the Vanilla Instant Pudding using the Milk.
Mix together the butter, cream cheese and 3/4 pkg Oreo Cookies.
Layer Cookie Mixture/Pudding Mixture.
Crumble the rest of the Oreo Cookies and put on the top. BUY SOME WORMS – Gummie Worms, that is.
Bury the worms randomly in the Top Layer of "Dirt."
Place a pretty *Gerber Daisy* or other cheerful flower into the Flower Pot.
Now, here's the good part: Bite the heads off the worms or chop them into little pieces with a cleaver. Whatever is your pleasure, do it. It's less risky than buying a gun.

CHAPTER 9

You Ignorant Slut

I looked at the Caller ID.

Bill Collector.

I picked up the phone and immediately replaced the receiver.

Within minutes, the phone rang again.

Let it go. Answering machine, pick up. Red blinking light.

I listened to the message. It took courage. I don't choose to hear bad news.

The recorded message was not good.

A threat. What's going on, I wondered.

My eyes stung.

"You ignorant slut," I thought to myself.

Chevy Chase's words to Jane Curtain wrap up the feelings I had about my inadequate perceptions on marriage. The words were often spoken after a segment on *SNL* when Jane Curtain was going on and on about certain factual situations and ole Chevy was just off camera mocking her with tongue-wagging, eye-rolling condescension, "Jane, you ignorant slut," he remarks and explains to her in arrogant tones. Ignorant is exactly what I felt. Slut is a relative term.

Looking back on the actions of a wayward husband brings plenty of pain. I was the one in the marriage who "hopes all things, believes all things." I was an enabling mess. Imagine these scenarios:

1. Receiving phone calls at 2 AM to ask if I know my husband's whereabouts,
2. Fielding calls from bill collectors,
3. Telling the children cover stories for the sake of their father, in his absence,
4. Tracking him to a bar when our son needed help on the highway.

And more.

The list of humiliations was unfathomable.

You may wonder why a mature woman would continuously accept this kind of behavior from her husband. I believed he was the man I married and he would eventually move out of this behavior, not move out of our home. The abrupt departure should not have been a total surprise. He had actually left the marriage years before he physically left the house.

In our church, Wednesday nights offered a variety of programming. One such six-week study focused on couples' relationships with a Christian family counselor leading the study. I attended each session, took notes, and tried to institute a number of the suggestions from the workshop text. While I asked my husband to attend with me, he refused, so I went by myself. There were quite a number of women there and several couples. Our text was written by Harville Hendrix with his wife Helen LaKelly Hunt and entitled *Getting the Love You Want*, originally published in 1988. The book focused on a unique process for couples, prospective couples, and parents. Doctors Hendrix and Hunt helped couples in their desire for "more loving, supportive, and deeply satisfying relationships." When I tried to share these insights, my husband told me not to bring it up again. And he was perturbed, to put it mildly.

Years later, after the cancer, I began seeing a Christian psychologist recommended by a precious friend. This man listened to my ramblings and asked all the right questions. He gave me writing exercises and visual cues to help me come to terms with my situation, both at home and at work. This wonder-worker heard some of my pain and asked, "Do you think you are going to divorce?"

In surprise, I answered, "Oh, no. We love each other."

He told me, "Just because you love each other does not mean you won't get a divorce. Couples divorce, even if they love each other."

That was the first time I ever considered that I might become a divorced person.

When I made a proposal about accompanying my ex on a business trip, he folded his hands and said, "No. Do not buy a ticket. I do not want you to go." I was trying to create the romantic reunion, the fairy-tale realization of what we were missing. The psychologist had recommended I make the overture and see where the chips would fall. They fell all over everything. I refused to recognize one fact: my marriage was over. The fire had been extinguished long before; the ashes lay cold and gray.

> *"Just because you love each other does not mean you won't get a divorce. Couples divorce, even if they love each other."*

I strongly suggest that you face your issues and whatever the outcome; accept it, deal with it, but don't blame yourself for holding on to the dream of a family intact. Sometimes, two people just cannot sustain enough of a viable relationship without destroying each other.

The destructive spiral that he has followed since the fateful day he left home has heaped pain on everyone involved. He paid child support for a few months, and then started bargaining with college funding promises.

There is no real gain when dealing with an individual who is thankful not to be responsible to anyone, for anything. When he left the life that most men dream of, he also left his conscience. Though some unfamiliar person walks around in the physical body of the man, this individual who now exists is, in many ways, a stranger to me. I know the essence of the man I married is there, somewhere, but his actions speak a foreign language I comprehend only in part.

The children, grown men now, have moved forward, though they are changed. When a child of whatever age believes he is a part of a secure, two-parent home and when that child wakes up the next morning to discover he is wrong, he is forever changed. Look squarely into their faces when considering divorce. However bad it will be for them, will remaining married make it worse, or will divorcing perhaps make it better? When a dream is lost, what can be gained? You may be happier, but they may not be happier at all. It will take every friend, relatives, every positive person and role model to help you influence and guide your children in their growing up. The "ex" can do what he can, but, as usual, it's up to Mama.

It would have been nice if the person I married had been the person I believed he was, because above all else I wish that my children had been spared the divorce. For me, however, there was no other route to take. I prayed for God to direct my footsteps. And, as always, He did.

I walked through the doors and down the path, trying not to trip on the boulders that littered the way.

Chapter 9 – You Ignorant Slut - Reflection:

The dreams you held for your married life died. You must grieve its death, but as you do, you will get through it and grow into happiness once again. You may feel that you wasted time and energy, placing faith in something that fell apart. You also lost someone you had loved enough to marry.

When two become one, how can a divorce be anything but a ripping and a tearing apart of the family? Discuss your insight about that concept.

"You either step forward into growth or you will step back into safety." – Abraham Maslow

Read the following scripture. Next, write a personal reflection about the meaning of each scripture for your life.

Proverbs 12: 22 – *"Lying lips are abomination to the Lord: but they that deal truly are his delight."*

Psalm 119:104 - *"Through thy precepts I get understanding; therefore I hate every false way."*

Tart Lesson: Dreams can dissolve.   *Sweet Pleasure: Looking squarely at truth brings freedom.*

Chapter 9 – You Ignorant Slut - Food for Thought:

Emotion is synonymous with cooking. Kitchen scenes in movies, even movies that focus on food itself, are popular. One scene that appeals to me contains a subtle sexiness. I refer to *Something to Talk About*. Julia Roberts had determined that Dennis Quaid had been having an affair. She made that clear at the Junior League meeting in down south horse country. She followed some advice and slipped dear hubby a dash of a potion in one of her drink creations when she invited him to supper to discuss their daughter. As he doubled over with unexplained pain later in the scene, Julia showed a sheepish grimace. Immediately remorseful, she rushed him to the hospital where he lost a few days and a few pounds. In the final scenes of the movie, the reconciliation begins in the kitchen with his preparation of dinner for two. He offers her a spoon to taste the sauce, at which time she cuts him a sly, "should I trust you?" look. The two laugh and we believe they will find this food their truce instead of their Waterloo.

Southern Cornbread Salad (this recipe begins with a very simple ingredient – a box or package of cornbread mix!)

    2 pkgs/boxes yellow cornbread mix such as Jiffy

(cook the cornbread according to recipe on the box! – just be sure there is no oil to be added)

3 med. tomatoes, chopped   1 ¾ c Miracle Whip
1 lg. bell pepper – chopped   4 – 6 slices crisp
1 cup onion – chopped   bacon – crumbled

Mix all ingredients. Crumble the baked cornbread and the bacon. Mix all together in a large bowl.
Cover and Refrigerate.

CHAPTER 10

Birthday Reality

The hot water tank leaked a rusty stream from the attic pipe and had been doing so for a while. I called the plumber, made friends with the company owner, and purchased a new water heater, lamenting that they came only in white. I hosted a hot water heater party. My friends knew I was at the end of my rope and bordering on instability, but they jumped right in and helped plan the menu. They agreed with my lament about water heaters; for that huge sum of money, there should be decorator colors.

We devoured 7-layer Mexican dip, BLT dip, chips, a vegie tray, and some liquid refreshment. Soon, it was time for a new take on decorator colors. Up to the attic we climbed, 2-3 girls at a time, gales of laughter wafting down the attic stairs. There, we decorated the water heater with markers, stickers, and stencils. I was a nut case, trying to do anything I could to add some levity to my situation. Thank goodness for very special girlfriends who went with me through it all. Like me, they vowed to maintain a sense of humor.

I had contacted the mortgage company and arranged for additional time and a payment schedule to catch up on the mortgage he left unpaid. You can do this, too. The mortgage company wants its money, however it can get the payment.

When I went into the file cabinets, I found stacks of bank statements unopened. I opened them, only to find no checks showing mortgage payments.

I had a good job, and I recalled asking him why we had no money. He'd become perturbed and mustered a good defense. I'd back off. I had been going through chemotherapy and I had good health insurance and supplemental cancer insurance, also. I could not figure it out. In those bad "we have no money" days, my dad helped me buy an oversize chair so I could rest from exhausting chemotherapy in the den.

Both car notes were mine as my job allowed for automatic deduction and since I had good credit, I was the one who paid those and all the health insurance. Additionally, one of the credit cards he was using was a joint card under my name. Using a credit card became a nerve racking experience because I was starting to get refusals and declines. I learned about a workshop for cleaning my credit. The credit counselors helped me find the credit reports and showed me how to refute the hits against my name that were actually hits against him. That took quite a while, but I got it done.

People will do to you what you allow, and continue, until you allow it no more.

Here is another suggestion: learn how to clean your credit, as I had to do. It is embarrassing, but must be done.

When I finally pulled open all the bank statements and put them in date order, I found that he had been writing checks for cash from our joint account for many months. I had not paid any attention, as I did not do much with the finances since the cancer diagnosis, surgeries, and treatments.

Money became my hot button. When I saw what I perceived as thievery, I called the bank. He had been cashing checks at a variety of places, including bars, and those places showed up with regularity. That was the kicker. Security for me was dependent on my job and my money, and he was taking both my money and, therefore, my security. I became furious. I had worked for so many years, providing stability for our family; he not only abandoned the family, he took money to fulfill his own scheme.

I got a lawyer. I met with a female lawyer and we talked a while before I hired her. She was a nice lawyer, one who was going to help me get through this thing. I did not really want to crucify him, as he did *quit claim* the house to me and I did want to set a good example for my boys. I was not going to put down their father in front of them, or make him appear to be so horrible.

Desertion. Betrayal. Infidelity. Various definitions. One meaning.

As the better part of valor, I chose "irreconcilable differences."

I should have hired a shark.

I filed for divorce on my birthday. I thought it was symbolic, rather like Martina McBride's *Independence Day*. But, he got a lawyer, too, one who recommended delay tactics to torment and frustrate me. The more back and forth the terms, the more money the lawyers got. Every phone call to my lawyer and to his cost me money. I finally became so frustrated, I just wanted it over. So, I ended it. Knowing I was somewhat over a barrel due to my job and level of income, I was tentative in pushing the law. It could backfire. Though he technically abandoned us, he had no real resources for me to attack. I was afraid I'd have to pay him.

As a defense, he said I had all the assets and I should pay for everything, all the bills and child-raising expenses. I had the assets plus the responsibility. While I did not want him put in jail, I had reached the furious level and secretly wanted him to wear cement shoes. But, he was still in the younger son's life, and I wanted that to work.

In the meantime, my dad and mom came to stay with me for a while. During that time, Dad guided me through making improvements around the house. The back yard had been neglected and was so overgrown that no one could see the partial fence or the steps up the terraced hill. Once the overgrowth was cleaned out, I rediscovered a nice back yard.

I spent a lot of time trying to keep peace in my life. Others wished to lead a search party to string up the scoundrel. I kept thinking about the boys and trying to conduct divorce business in a civilized manner. Murder committed by my dad would not help things along very much.

Even though he left the marriage, I filed for the divorce. I initiated the legal action when I was emotionally ready to do so. The action coming from me was an appropriate response on my part, and did allow me to gain strength from the process.

As it turned out, we did keep it civilized and respectful, but he did not fulfill his end of the obligation. Child support evaporated. I could have garnished his wages, at which time he would either quit his job or get fired from it. I could have sent him in jail, but to what end. Then, how would he get a job and have any money to support his child? I was in a dilemma. How, I wondered, could he be such an ass in one regard, and a decent human being in another. I guess we all have those dichotomous conflicts within us. In retrospect, I should have fought for the money and banked it for the future. Hind-sight.

I found that I had more money, single and on one income than I had married on two incomes. I was not as lonesome as one might think, as I had been lonesome for so long and had felt abandoned, that when the solo venture became a reality, it was just life as usual, but I did not have to worry about what time he might come in at night. I did not have to be at home at any particular time and my son and I could set our schedule as we wanted. I felt "set free." I'm sure he did, too. I experienced a different kind of "birth-day."

Chapter 10 – Birthday Reality - Reflection:

Discuss the phrase "dichotomous conflicts within us." How might that phrase apply in your situation?

Read the following scripture. Next, write a personal reflection about the meaning of each scripture for your life.

Ephesians 4: 31-32 – *"Let all bitterness, and wrath, and anger, and clamour, and evil speaking, be put away from you, with all malice; And be ye kind one to another, tenderhearted, forgiving one another, even as God for Christ's sake hath forgiven you."*

Jeremiah 29: 11 – *"For I know the thoughts that I think toward you, saith the Lord, thoughts of peace, and not of evil, to give you an expected end."*

Tart Lesson: A man you trusted can betray you.   Sweet Pleasure: Self-worth is hugely important.

Chapter 10 – Birthday Reality - Food for Thought:

Movies that bring to mind culinary scenes with a generous sprinkling of humor include *Mrs. Doubtfire* and *Christmas Vacation* with Chevy Chase. Most unfortunate and previously uninvolved father, Robin Williams, was hired as Nanny to his own children. Sally Field, the children's mother, dates again and Mrs. Doubtfire volunteers to prepare supper and babysit the kids. Hilarity flowed as Mrs. Doubtfire (Robin Williams in drag) uses two pot-lids to extinguish flames on protruding hoochie-coochies as he watches the supper erupt in flames.

Then, we must recall the sad state of affairs at Christmas dinner when Chevy Chase's (Clark Griswold) intact family tasted the culinary treat of lime Jell-o mold with cat litter and a dried out turkey containing only morsels of meat baked onto the brittle bones with no hint of moisture, except escaping steam. The dog rummaging the trash fared better.

Mixed up, crazy families are not limited to families experiencing divorce. Families by their very nature are "crazy."

Coconut Pie (I'd rather have coconut pie than birthday cake.)

¾+ cup sugar	Pinch salt
2T+ Cornstarch	3T butter
2 C milk (or Half-Half)	2+ t vanilla
3 large eggs –yolk (save whites for meringue)	1 cup coconut

Let cooked custard stand 30 min. Spoon into prepared/pre-baked pie crust. Chill for 30 minutes.
Top with meringue which has stiff peaks. Sprinkle with coconut flakes. Run this into the oven briefly to brown the tips.

Chapter 11

Big Bad Wolf Insurance

In the ideal world, the marriage vows would be sacred for all. As a Christian, you trusted that your marriage vows would sustain you through war, pestilence, famine, fire, and for better or worse. Our priorities are upended and to be prudent, we must consider divorce as a possibility, even in lifetime Christian marriages. If not divorce, the possibility of a woman raising children alone is no more foreign now than it was in our grandmothers' era. The difference is the strength of the family. That former resource is gone, for the most part. Women become vulnerable without another kind of insurance.

I have read of divorce insurance and prenuptial contracts. Those concepts are worthy of consideration when marrying later in life when you are in a different financial and child-raising position. But, this is not the *Big Bad Wolf Insurance* to which I refer. This *BBW* Insurance I suggest that you acquire from the beginning of your adult life. Much of it has to do with an attitude of action.

My position on Big Bad Wolf Insurance makes this supposition: BBW Insurance is your best insulation from "the worst that could happen." It gives you options instead of tying your hands. BBW Insurance, especially for women, is found in only a few places: Education and Job Training with options for employment beyond minimum wage.

If you happen to join the ranks of statistical mayhem in this country, invest in insurance for your family through an attitude of forward planning and hard work.

Without BBW Insurance, women are relegated to dead marriages, abusive relationships, and remain trapped because the man provides financially, and these women can't provide for the family alone. It's contrary to God's plan for the family, but it's today's reality. Without BBW Insurance, these mothers and their children become dependent on either the State or grandparents, or both.

Trusting God to guide you in taking precautions and making smart choices is a part of having responsibility for yourself and your children. Trust God to guide you in these decisions; listen to the gentle urgings and follow through with what God is telling you. He is opening and closing doors, helping you establish good relationships. You must pray, though. And you must listen. Then, act.

I was prepared, though not "in case of divorce." I had the means to provide a better life for my family. Education did not keep the divorce wolf from climbing atop my roof, but it helped me build the fire and boil that wolf's behind in a fiery kettle as he fell down my chimney. My life and my options would have been much different without my education and my career.

I found that I had more money, single, with one income than I had married, with two.

My mother did not work outside the house, so she could not understand why I continued in my profession, even after the kids came. I had a very clear feeling that I needed to continue being proactive with my career, and I wanted to do that. It was personally fulfilling and satisfying to my ego. The personal satisfaction and "strokes" filled a void.

I did not know how important my job would be to me and my children as that unforeseen wolf huffed and puffed at my door. You might recall how Noah began to build the Ark when not a cloud was in the sky!

BBW Insurance can also be in the form of wonderful, loyal friends, a totally supportive church and church fellowship, youth groups for your children, and open communication with your parents, if they are still living. None of these things can suddenly appear in your life. It's very important that you not live in isolation, building your home on sinking sand, out of straw and sticks. Do not try to survive this messiness alone.

BBW Insurance includes a second form of preparation if divorce is imminent: hire a really good lawyer who will be tough and firm when you are ready to give up and cry, throw in the towel and say *whatever*. You also need a good job; if you don't have a job, get some training, and get back into the work force, as soon as you are able. Now, if the soon-to-be ex has money, you need a good lawyer to get your fair share. And if you have a good job, investigate a plan to protect your financial position.

Here you are, a fine Christian in a position you never in a million years imagined for yourself. How can this mess fit with your concept of Christianity? What is it about Faith that seems to imply we are to do nothing and leave it all to God? There are those persons who profess that we should "let go and let God" and they do just that…they sit down and do nothing, claiming great Faith. What are we to do when we pick up on warning signs? What does God have to say about preparation for possibilities, probabilities, even disaster? Does he tell us to sit down and do nothing to protect ourselves and our families?

I said I was blindsided; I was not. There are always warning signs, nudges from God to pay attention. Thoughts rambled within my brain, but I justified and explained away everything. There were plenty of clues. An internal warning system is in place and, like everything else, we must be in tune with what is happening. We have a choice to ignore, disregard, claiming *this, too, shall pass*. Or, when something does not sit right, when we have that intuition, remember, it's not a fluke or indigestion; it's God. Listen to Him.

We prefer our status quo. We will hold on to *like it's always been* even if what might be much better is right before us. In doing the comfortable thing, we may ignore warning signs, headlights, and not realize what is imminent, what is coming around the next corner.

"Would you tell me which way I ought to go from here?" asked Alice. "That depends a good deal on where you want to get," said the Cat. "I really don't care where," replied Alice. "Then it doesn't much matter which way you go," said the Cat. - Lewis Carroll, novelist and poet (1832-1898), <u>Alice's Adventures in Wonderland</u> (1865).

In Genesis, Noah is told to prepare and build the Ark. God had told Noah that there was 100% chance of rain in his area. Noah could have just stayed put, done nothing, and escaped ridicule. Instead, he prepared. Noah did not *let go and let God.* He *acted* in Faith. He *obeyed* God and *followed God's lead* with action.

> *I said I was blindsided;*
> *I was not.*

In Exodus, Joseph dreamed and told folks to prepare, to get ready, take care of family. He advised everyone to put grain in the storehouses, because even in the midst of the feast, one should prepare for the famine. People scoffed. But he stored up plenty for himself, and even for his family, his brothers. He acted on what God showed him in a dream. He had faith in God to have given him the dream and the plan.

Refusal to act does not honor God's activity in our lives.

Make wise decisions to take care of yourself and your family. God is setting opportunity before you; please pay attention and act. We must make some very wise decisions because we will need dollars… and sense.

In my life and in yours, there have been and will continue to be tornadoes, hurricanes, earthquakes, and recessions, even depressions as we have faced recently. Divorce is more devastating to your family than those disasters, especially if you have no BBW Insurance, no plans, no preparation to meet this particular calamity head on and come out successful and whole.

Chapter 11 – Big Bad Wolf Insurance - Reflection:

Read the following scripture. Next, write a personal reflection about the meaning of each scripture for your life.

Proverbs 24: 3-4- "Through wisdom is an house builded; and by understanding it is established: And by knowledge shall the chambers be filled with all precious and pleasant riches."

Tart Lesson: Without conscious preparation, you will be caught flat-footed.

Sweet Pleasure: Your life's Outcome is Your Responsibility under the leadership of God.

Chapter 11 – Big Bad Wolf Insurance - Food for Thought:

The original Disney version of *The Parent Trap* starring Haley Mills, Maureen O'Hara, and Brian Keith placed the divorced parents in his California kitchen, preparing spaghetti. The scene led to their reconciliation. Only Disney's animated gem *Lady and the Tramp* could possibly be more romantic and involve spaghetti.

If it's possible to reconcile with your husband, in a way healthy for you, I believe you should do that. But, the reality often not portrayed in movies is that you will not reconcile in his mansion in California over a plate of spaghetti, nor will you marry Prince Charming who has been scouring the countryside with your missing shoe, thus rescuing you from a life "in a van down by the river."

Millionaire's Salad (Prepare financially for the future)

1 pkg lime jello (the Color of Money)	2 pkgs softened cream cheese
	Mini marshmallows
1 c water	1 cup pecans
½ pt xxx cream (whipped) or Cool Whip	1 sm can crushed pineapple

Mix jello with water and let stand until syrupy. Then, mix all together. Chill until congealed.

Chapter 12

Waiting for the Next Mr. Wrong

Peer Pressure: It's not just for teenagers, anymore. I gave in to the peer pressure and went clubbing with single girlfriends. I gulped reassurance from their encouragement and joined them at a local dance club, against my better judgment. I was hit on by a painter; not a Renaissance man, not even close to Monet or Picasso, though he did have a body part missing: part of a finger rather than a portion of ear. He was a house painter who wore gold chains and sported black hairs peeking from his shirt.

It was those black hairs peeking with wiry intentions that convinced me to wait longer to date. In spite of our instant lifestyle and our dislike for waiting, life is full of chances for waiting. And one of the most challenging exhortations of Scripture is *Wait*.

After five years of living divorced, I put my fears aside and entered the dating scene: time to discover who is available at age 50-ish. My sons participated by informing me that my wardrobe needed an overhaul. I thought the boots and long black skirt with long sweater was up-to-date. "You look like a Pilgrim." Seems my style was a tad outdated, but a Pilgrim? I went shopping immediately to bait the trap with a more glamorous look.

I would date, but remain single before attaching to any man who could not provide something positive to my life. That truth I learned while studying and sharing in a Divorce Recovery workshop. Why would I date someone who took without giving, who needed me to take care of him, emotionally or financially? I had already lived that for one lifetime.

Hopefully, the goofballs in dating land play in someone else's sandbox.

However right any of us might be, we are flawed; we are filled with weaknesses and troubles, baggage and junky lives. That's the way God made us. We have to join forces with Him so that we can live with our faults and with the faults of others. We are all Mr. /Ms Wrong. But we can be right to the right person.

Realizing that my church, like most family-centered mainline churches, was filled with married couples and very few single people, I visited a mega-church. One of the first arenas I explored was a singles class. I found a multitude of much younger single men and women. In the older group were quite a few divorced gentlemen who remained single *for a reason,* let me point out.

Feeling emotionally stronger, I decided it was time to dip a toe into the digital age: *yourperfectmatch.com*. So many permanent older frogs are on the web, begging to be kissed. Most of them want one thing only and it's not a conversation. One guy kept emailing to ask if I wanted to go for the weekend to his cabin in the woods. I think he forgot that I told him *no*, so he kept sending the emails. The site continued to show my profile as single and to him, I was still available.

Another route to the dating scene was *e-heart-song*, promising a personality profile and the ability to connect with my soul mate. The person(s) set up as my soul mates did contact me, but several were out of my geographic area. A couple of us tried to set up some meetings, but I was not willing to travel to the casino, or meet a plane from a bordering state since I was never really sure who was on the other end of the email; the Web, regardless of promises, is filled with deceit.

One gentleman was a professional in the health-care industry, and was painfully shy. While we shared numerous interests and were both professional adults, he exhausted me as I tried to keep the conversation going. Finally, he held my hand and kissed me, which left me cold. Clearly, while the paperwork indicated a match, neither of us felt the spark of mutual attraction.

A really spooky man had a style that seemed to work for a while. He was quite adept at writing e-mails; soon I realized he took portions of my profile and my responses and wove the information into his e-mails to show how simpatico we were. When we began to talk on the phone, I asked questions and the answers did not have the tone contained in the emails. I found out that he lived in a tiny apartment with a huge dog, was a pizza delivery man, and learned about playing bridge from delivering pizzas to a ladies bridge club. Luckily, I did not meet him at all and we never exchanged much information. I also told him that if he called me again, I would turn his name over to the police. That put a stop to his phone calls.

Friends also gave my name to some of their acquaintances. I went out with a man who said he wanted a good woman. I felt way too young and cute to be anyone's good woman. I pictured me, the "good woman" in a housedress and orthopedic shoes. I did not go out with him again.

I also considered speed dating, encouraged by a friend in my neighborhood. When I saw all the side-cars parked in front of the posted venue, I never sent in my registration fee.

Even in the triage area of a local hospital where I took my mother who was suffering from a fractured pelvis, there was an opportunity for male-female attraction. A male triage nurse wanted to take me for coffee and get my phone number. Mother encouraged me to act brave, but brave is one thing; stupid is altogether different.

I dated casually, and went to a couple of singles outings and parties. Most of the men were considerably younger than I and all of them on the prowl. The single women also prowled and dressed quite provocatively. So, with all that confronting me as reality, I said, "Oh, well. I am through with the matching web sites, the e-promises, and all the other searchers on the scene."

My journey and my quest are not unique. Stories such as mine are everywhere, in countless women's magazines and in the produce section of the neighborhood grocery store. The men I encountered were Mr. Right to other women, just not for me. The difference, determined in retrospection, is that what I share with you is double-edged. It is not only my answered prayer, but his, as well. I hope that something shared here provide inspiration to you in trusting God to open the doors for you. We should stop our attempts to find Mr./Ms Right. If we are concentrating on becoming Mr./Ms Right, our counterpart will be led to us.

> *However "right" any of us might be, we are flawed; we are filled with weaknesses and troubles, baggage and junky lives.*

Then, one afternoon, I was reading my email and noticed an encouraging comment from the Christian Singles group I had joined. By then, I had followed a crazy neighbor and had joined the local club. I clicked on the web site and read my messages, all two of them. I replied, by saying thanks, but no thanks. Then, on a whim, I glanced at the multitude (read: ten) of men in the 50 – 60 age range. All of them I had seen before – except for one man.

He had hair. He had a nice smile, clever eyes, his face was clean shaven; he was neither deformed nor fat, at least not in his picture. Besides that, it appeared from his profile that he had a job.

J-O-B! Chalk up a bonus point for the guy. He was in the right age range, so I would not have to explain that Paul McCartney was in a singing group before *Wings*. This man had to submit to a background check to be a member of this group and I knew the questions in the interview. So, I felt that he probably was not an axe murderer, another bonus point- that's 2 points, total. A man who signed up with this group had some basic values that were compatible with mine. Add to that, he was not only taller than I, he was tall enough for me to wear my really high heels – so, that's a total of 3 points! This person was worth an email, so that's what I did. Nice, sweet, and non-committal, "Write back if you want to."

I got a reply and he asked for my phone number. What the heck, I just gave him every number I had, except for my bank account. He called, we talked, decided to meet at the mall on a Saturday afternoon.

I'll confess that I stood beside a potted plant on the side opposite the entrance, ready to disappear should he weigh 100 pounds more than his picture suggested, ready to vanish if he posted a "before" picture, before he had received a bashing with the ugly stick. I was nervous. He walked in. I liked what I saw and came from behind the carousel and walked up to him, hoping he'd like me, too.

We talked for over two hours. He seemed captivated by my personality, by my ease in conversation. I focused on him and asked him questions that were open-ended. He talked. I listened. What a relief – someone who liked to talk as much as I. So, in listening, I became a fabulous conversationalist. I wondered if he would ever stop talking and listen to me. We wore out every bench in the mall, sitting, talking, moving on, neither ready to leave, but not sure if going forward was the answer either.

Over the next few weeks he asked me to join him for a movie, for dinner, and I was willing to do that, because it was a social life I was looking for, nothing more. His sense of humor added an additional point of attractiveness. He could hold his own with conversational, good-natured banter, and to me, that's a turn-on.

There was a down-side. I hesitated because he had some rough edges that caused me to be leery. Girlfriends suggested that I "cut the guy some slack."

God must have been in these first meetings. I was interested enough to let him lead the way to determine how much time we'd give each other. He must have been following God's lead, also, because instead of walking away from someone like me, someone unlike anyone he had ever dated, he was fascinated, intrigued, and interested. He began his pursuit, at least for a few dates, to see how it went. I enjoyed the attention.

His search had followed a similar track, in that he had been taken for disastrous rides via the internet. Loneliness had its way. He had joined the same Christian singles group as a social outreach. Now, he had met me and he was interested but I was different. Reaching out to take his hand as we walked, I slipped my little palm right into his. He had not responded in any way, so I doubted he liked me very much but he enjoyed talking with someone who was first and foremost female. I had my own job, my own income. I was not a dependent female he should rescue. With my independence, men are often intimidated: not so, this man.

It seems that I was right, for he soon told me that he had concerns about me. He wondered if any chemistry might exist. He continued to confess that he had always felt immediate sexual chemistry with the other women in his life, so I was a mystery. He really liked me, but he was not chasing me around the parking lot.

When a guy tells a girl this bit of information, she'd just as soon sink into the ground. It's quite an ego-bruiser since we have a wish to set his heart aflame. While we look cute and flutter our eyelashes, some of us do not give away the candy and certainly not the entire store. We learned that at our mother's knee. I summonsed my new-found feminine ego and sighed. The concern he voiced rang the *deja vu* bell.

It takes strong self-worth to turn, get into the car, and say thank you for the nice dinner, not knowing if he will call again. If that's the way it ends, so be it. This is who I am, and I will not play at being who I am not. Better to end it now, after a few dates and no attachments, than later, when hurt could possibly be in the cards. After the emotional wreckage from my marriage, and months in Divorce Recovery, I'd emerged with a sure sense of who I am and I'd accepted myself.

I told him, "Well, you have to do what feels right for you. This is who I am."

And it could have ended that very night but it didn't.

I was surprised when he continued to call me. As I said, something was driving this relationship through both of us, not just one of us. Both of us were interested enough to give the other a little time, because of the conversation, the wit, the personalities.

Had it been another year, another place, another situation, would we have met or even gone on a date? I have no way of knowing. However, we did meet, and felt strongly that we should not say goodbye too quickly. Both of us decided to follow the path and see where the road would lead.

Chapter 12 – Waiting for the Next Mr. Wrong - Reflection:

Being true to yourself can happen if you WAIT to DATE. The rule of thumb is 1 year WAITING for every 5 years of marriage. Actually, that is the rule of thumb for serious relationships. But, given that men want to get serious very quickly, if you are dating, you are subject to getting pulled in when you are not ready. Men don't wait.

List the reasons you should WAIT to DATE. Sometimes, dating just to enjoy an outing with NO expectations can bolster your ego. Don't go into the date wondering how long it will take him to propose, or if he'll be a good daddy. Just enjoy his company. WAIT and then, WAIT Longer.

"Never give up, for that is just the place and time that the tide will turn." –Harriet Beecher Stowe

List the areas you need to work on <u>to be a good mate</u>, a good partner in a relationship.

Read the following scripture. Next, write a personal reflection about the meaning of each scripture for your life.

Isaiah 40:31 - *"But they that wait upon the Lord shall renew their strength; they shall mount up with wings as eagles; they shall run, and not be weary; and they shall walk, and not faint."*

Tart Lesson: Dating desperate men may be inevitable.   Sweet Pleasure: Waiting is valuable.

Chapter 12 – Waiting for the Next Mr. Wrong
Food for Thought:

Culinary seduction can be sensuously rewarding. Not like Mickey Rourke in *9 ½ Weeks*, my man could cook and not pour food on me. He wooed me with comfort food and ice cream by candlelight. We shared peach cobbler during our slow and steamy Sunday dinners. Comfort foods, healthy dishes, sweet treats and dim lighting whispered "I Love You." We have cooked together, but it is my special pleasure to cook for him since he is a hugely appreciative diner. His remarks about how wonderful a cook I am ramp up my desire to prepare dishes for him that are even tastier.

To men, a woman who can cook signals not only her creativity but her love and ultimately, her sexiness. "The only thing better than a beautiful woman is a beautiful woman who can **cook**." We should embrace the sexiness and sensuality inherent in preparation of a romantic dinner for our lovers.

HOT CHICKEN SALAD (He was hot stuff to me)

2 cups diced chicken
1 can cream of chicken soup
1 cup finely diced celery
2 Tbs minced onion
1/2 cup lightly toasted slivered almonds
1/2 cup mayonnaise
1/2 tsp each salt and pepper
2 Tbs lemon juice
3 hard boiled eggs – sliced

Mix All Together
Top with Ruffles (sturdy) potato chips and grated cheddar cheese
Bake at 350 degrees for 25 minutes in 13x9 casserole dish

CHAPTER 13

Dancing With Frogs

Bring in men who are willing to dance with someone whose fur is rubbed off in splotchy patterns, as in *The Velveteen Rabbit* – someone who is real. Many single or divorced men seek the trophy-wife or girlfriend who magically turned from a life as a porn star to become the girl they can take home to Mama. She needs to be Julia Roberts in *Pretty Woman*, a girl of his fantasy. He is the twin of Richard Gere who finds Vivian Ward on his pillow.

A fear second only to rejection and linked to it – will we ever really love again? Some women take the phrase and have coined, "I'd rather fall into chocolate" as their mantra. Some women shut down the system of feelings in all departments. We know that's what we did, because it is so much easier. Just shut it all down like Luke Skywalker screamed to R2D2, "Shut down all the trash compactors on the detention level – shut them all down!" Don't think about it, don't read about it, and certainly don't watch that happily-ever-after program on television.

We find denial easier and easier as the months and years go by – easier to deny our emotional longings than to accept them. We become tougher, almost hardened, our demeanor rigid. We put away the silk and pull out the flannel for insulation. We plan on celebrating our wallflower status.

God knows fear when He confronts it in mankind. After all, what did the Angel recognize in Mary, the young, unmarried woman, when she was approached with the life-changing announcement of the birth of our Savior and her role in this miracle?

And, the simple shepherds out minding their own business felt fear. They were accustomed to watching for predators desiring to feast on the sheep, but to be awakened by an Angel? That Angel and her heavenly chorus announced to the shepherds watching the little lambs sleeping on the hillside. God intervened in humankind and told us all the same thing: Do not be afraid. God breaks into our lives like that, still. We all need reminding of God's hand in our lives as we wonder about the second part of our adult lives.

We are the little dreamy girls who saw *Snow White* and *Cinderella* on the big screen and dressed up like these princesses on Halloween. We are the Barbie generation who always wanted Barbie and Ken to marry. We saved our allowances to buy the Wedding Ensemble. We are the 60's teenagers who still know the words to the Golden Oldies songs about true love. We smiled as Tammy snagged the Bachelor. We giggled with Gidget and her ultimate hunk Moondoggie. We even watched Tiny Tim and Miss Vickie tiptoe through the tulips on the *Johnny Carson Show*. We invested our whole lives, our very essence, in a fairy-tale, life-long marriage. Somehow, it didn't work out.

A broken heart can be healed, because it wants so desperately to love again.

God knows life is not perfect, which is why Jesus was sent to walk among us. Are we going to continue to be afraid of rejection, loneliness, and ultimately, love, fearing that this experience won't be perfect? Are we going to get bogged down in the mess of life and miss what God has in store for us?

We must recognize that there are some things we are powerless to change and we need to stop bemoaning and reliving the past. We have one wonderful advantage in our situation: We have God at our side and He is saying to us, "Do Not Be Afraid; I will use your strife, anguish, and broken heart to bring you a life better than before – better than the one you had or the one you might have planned for." Put down the road maps and surrender to following His lead. You need nothing except direction from God and the ability to follow through with action.

How will I know whether the current journey is God's plan? Remember, God is not only working for me and you, He is working for that unknown man, or perhaps one who is already known to you, bringing into his life what he needs, also. Following the leads and walking through the open doors is a much easier way of living than beating down locked doors and ramming fists and heads through thick walls of resistance.

A person might have a strong fear of failure, or self-doubt. Such doubt would have kept Annie Sullivan from rescuing Helen Keller. It would have grounded the astronauts and kept brilliant musicians and artists from bestowing beauty to our world. If we don't believe in ourselves or our worth, we will be unable to bestow our gifts upon loved ones and this hesitancy would keep us from seeing the beauty the world has to offer. Faith comes from God; He believes in us, His children. God gives us the ability to make good decisions. He is whispering now.

Even though I was operating in unfamiliar territory, I had a strange desire to stay where I was, though I could have walked out at any time. I had to decide. It was faith in the guiding hand of God in my life. It was faith to recognize the goodness in a person and sift through the rough, scratchy sand to find the seashell upon the shore. I have taken the chance at happiness and love. "Loving may be a mistake, but it's worth making," a line I borrow from LeAnn Womack's words "when you get the chance to sit it out or dance, *I Hope You Dance*."

Chapter 13 – Dancing With Frogs - Reflection:

Take it slow and easy, experience all the seasons, breathe the same air, learn each other, pray for one another – how important time becomes when learning about each other. Reflect and write your response.

Read the following scripture. Next, write a personal reflection about the meaning of each scripture for your life.

James 5: 16 – *"Confess your faults one to another, and pray one for another, that ye may be healed. The effectual fervent prayer of a righteous man availeth much."*

Tart Lesson: Mistakes are inevitable.   Sweet Pleasure: Faith in the opposite sex may be restored.

Chapter 13 – Dancing With Frogs - Food for Thought:

A recipe everyone uses and many bake regularly is the one I claimed as my own creation. It is my "signature" cake.

It was the first cake I made on my own as a collegian. I introduced it to my family.

While our paths are directed by God, we design our steps and fashion our turns, living individually with our own signature on living.

Perhaps it was the blend of sweet and tart that drew me to claim it, the combination that inspired me. It became "me."

Signature Lemon Cake (I'll share this favorite cake and share my life.)

1 pkg lemon velvet cake mix	1 c water
1 pkg lemon instant pudding	4 eggs
¾ cup oil	

Put first 5 ingredients in bowl and mix until well blended. Pour into a well-greased and floured pan (13 ½ x 8 x 2 ½). Bake at 325 degrees for about 35-40 min. Remove from oven and prick all over with a fork and pout on the following glaze.

Glaze: 2 c sifted powdered sugar (XXX) + 1/3 c lemon juice

Bonus- For gingerbread or Mother's Easy Pound Cake, this Lemon Sauce is better than any you could buy, even in a gourmet shop. Some recipes call this treat "lemon curd," as it will set up and thicken, keeping for weeks, covered in the refrigerator.

Lemon Sauce (The essence of lemon brings a sweet and tart flavor to many dishes.)

½ c butter	1 T lemon juice
1 c sugar	1 T grated lemon peel (can use
¼ c water	*Penzey's*)
1 egg well-beaten	

Mix all ingredients and cook over medium heat, stirring constantly, until mixture comes to boiling.

This sauce can be poured or spooned onto gingerbread, pound cake, or other desserts.

CHAPTER 14

Carousel Ride

And I walked around the carousel and straight into the rest of my life.

The meeting at the mall was intriguing, and I had a sense of safety with this particular man because of the Christian connection. Conversations that began on that afternoon were an interesting challenge, entertaining, and fun. We interrupted each other so often that I wondered if we heard what the other was saying. We were anxious to talk; we'd listen, poised on the edge of sound, waiting for a brief silence while the other took a breath, ready to have a turn. The lively conversations were quick paced, humorous, and mentally stimulating, rather like watching stand-up comedians with a practiced pitch and catch routine. However, I had no expectation that anything would come from this initial meeting, though a dinner date or movie would be fun.

I cannot remember a single thing we talked about that afternoon, but I learned enough that I hoped for a second meeting. The second meeting did come and the conversations continued. At no time during our relationship have we been unable to talk about, debate, discuss whatever the issue.

How common it is and how sad it would have been had we made a hurried decision to pounce on our dividing points. Our backgrounds are different, but our upbringing is similar. Our education is different, but our ambition and resulting success are quite similar, he in his field, I in mine. Our religious denominations differ, but our Christian understanding was the same. Our needs are similar, our hopes the same.

Society examines dividing elements much more often than commonalities. Only through God's presence in our hearts were we able to see past the frayed edges worn rough through broken hearts and betrayed dreams. There is something so wonderful about the human spirit – the spirit that keeps hoping, keeps believing.

This story is of hope, love, and inspiration. Contained here is a depiction of God continuing to shower His children with gifts in ways we never dreamed and from places we had chosen to forget. This story of divine timing illustrates that when we least expect God's generous hand, when we are busy doing other things, He reaches into our hearts and minds and reminds us to – give it up – quit trying to lead. He knows exactly what we want, need and desire. He asks that we trust, believe, listen, and follow His lead, walking through open doors. Unlike the five-year quality of our own plans, God's plan results in life which is better than we could imagine.

In the early years, after the unthinkable divorce, I believed I didn't need anyone or anything. I owned my own leaf-blower, power screwdriver, and had a membership to AAA (Triple A). I possessed a big power light for scaring away thunderstorms, tornados, hurricanes, and ice storms. I had taken self-defense classes and was capable of raising the hood on my car. The Force was with me; Yoda noticed me in possession of a Millennium Falcon emergency roadside assistance kit.

But, with all this power, I still feared rejection. The divorce itself rejected the dream of our intact family seated around the holiday dinner tables- even if it's like the Grizwold's grab-bag gathering on Christmas Day. The vision of the grandmother and grandfather stirring around the kitchen together, kicking back in matching recliners, waiting for the grandchildren to visit – however simple a dream that was – it is over- discarded along with yesterday's newspaper and trendy fashions.

Divorce is a failure, no matter what we use to justify the situation. Life happened. None of us is immune to life and its failures. That is what John Lennon told us: "Life is what happens to us while we are busy making other plans." Our loving Father-God can and will use hurtful events in our lives to make us into stronger women/men. He is the one with the Power.

The lonely nights invade and we would seek to hide in sweatpants and baggy shirts, holding the remote control. We hide in endless activity. After the completion of our night rituals, when we turn off the lights, delayed as long as possible, the bed is huge and the house is too quiet. The dark loneliness seeps into our bones and gives us crazy thoughts.

> *"The gem cannot be polished without friction nor perfected without trials." - Unknown*

We girls must be careful not to gravitate to troops of divorced women. Remember the female sharing session in the sister's living room with Tom Cruise in *Jerry McGuire*? If it were not for Renee' Zellweger's statement that she "still loves the enemy," the group would self-destruct into a man-bashing garbage-fest of colossal proportions. We must eliminate those people who are discouraging us and throwing us into the abyss. We need reminders of the goodness in life, not sessions of abject negativity.

God wants nothing but good things for His children who love and serve Him. While He condemns divorce, He knows and feels our pain, suffering, and guilt. He walked among us in human form. He remembers us and our prayers. He bestows mercy on those of us who stayed when the staying wasn't good at all. It's worth everything to acknowledge God's provision in the desert. If "risk" is the word, then do it: be quiet and listen for God's whisper.

The bumper sticker proclaims that God is the co-pilot. That belief defies Christian understandings. God pilots; God drives. I've trusted roadmaps which I cannot read accurately. I've depended on passengers to tell me when to exit; they are as involved in the conversation as I and we drive right past. The pathways of our lives are littered with distractions: large balls of twine and jack-a-lopes. Oh, what time we waste sightseeing within our own life.

Chapter 14 – Carousel Ride - Reflection:

List characteristics of men you wish to avoid in your next romance.

What are the traits about each person you considered as a potential mate?

List characteristics in your next man <u>that would make you</u> a better, stronger person, characteristics that would edify you.

List qualities you desire in your next husband/partner.

Read the following scripture. Next, write a personal reflection about the meaning of each scripture for your life.

James 1: 17 – *"Every good gift and every perfect gift is from above, and cometh down from the Father of lights, with whom is no variableness, neither shadow of turning."*

Tart Lesson: Fear is inevitable.   Sweet Pleasure: Risk is worth it.

Chapter 14 – Carousel Ride - Food for Thought:

Fatal Attraction starring Michael Douglas, Anne Archer, and Glenn Close as the fateful triad allowed us to gape into the life of the tempted husband and the psycho who *can't get no satisfaction*. Fear was portrayed throughout this movie. The kind of risk that Michael Douglas' character took is not the risk that can bring anything good: successful married man succumbs to one weekend of temptress passion beginning with a remark, "Have you ever done it in an elevator?" The lesson underlines our cultural belief that affairs are wrong – see what they'll get you? Bring in sex on the counter and the boiling bunny and you've got plenty of reasons to avoid the kitchen. When Michael Douglas fails to drown the knife wielding and bloody Glenn Close, Wife walks in. Wife brings a gun to the knife fight and we realize that *fatal attractions* are fatal, indeed.

PINEAPPLE UPSIDE DOWN CAKE (What your current life will be like after risk. A risk does not have to constitute an affair; it could be two adventurous spirits soaring after a delicious yet exhausting encounter!" Hunger in its many forms can be satisfied. The second way is with this dessert, concocted that very night.")

1 T butter
¼ c. brown sugar
3 slices Pineapple, cut in half
Handful of pecan halves
3 eggs – separate into yolks and whites
½ c. sugar

Sift together: ½ t baking powder and 1/8 t salt ½ c pre-sifted regular baking flour/all-purpose flour
3 T water
½ t vanilla

Melt butter in cake pan
Add brown sugar, pineapple and pecans
Beat egg whites 'til stiff
Add egg yolks and continue beating, gradually adding sugar.

E. J. Gordon

Fold in sifted flour

Add baking powder and salt which have been sifted together.
Add water and vanilla.

Pour over pineapple.
Bake at 325 degrees for about 30 minutes.
Serves 4- or- a really hungry couple in the kitchen at midnight.

Chapter 15

Roadmaps, Roadblocks, and Stop Signs

"She kept getting in my space and putting her hands on me. Giving me these looks. Leaning forward. We went to supper, but I took her to *Danvers* for a quick sandwich. I was so nervous with her. After 15 minutes, I kept looking at my watch; I was ready to get out of there, get as far away from her as I could," he confided. (I smiled.) I had told him to go ahead with his previous plans.

"I couldn't wait to see you and tell you about it. Can I come over?"

(Sure, Red Rover, Come on over!)

Right up in my personal space breathed a man unlike anyone I had ever dated. However, this man could answer "yes" to a number of my checklist requirements. The personality is vital, the strength of character and values are critical. So, this man has all of that, and I am questioning whether to simply tell him my concerns and let the chips fall where they may or just say "you're a great person, but…"

What I did was give the situation a "wait and see" framework. I decided to wait for the message to come to me, not in a bottle, but in a clear and specific way from God. I had experienced enough of God's guidance to know that the way to go would be clearly placed before me. Doing something as hasty as closing doors that are barely open was not a wise thing to do. Kicking this guy to the curb was not a good plan. Insisting he be perfect while allowing myself to remain flawed…that was not going to work.

I was watching television that Saturday evening, having worked around the house and in the yard all day, no make-up, shorts, basically "au natural." After what must have been an hour for him at the dinner with another lady, the caller ID indicated that it was he calling. Seems the dinner was not at all what he wanted and he asked to come over since he was half way to my house anyway. While I was flattered, I was also hesitant. I thought it odd that he knew generally where I lived, since I had not given him my address. I was a little spooked, but he promised not to stay long, and actually pled - just wanted to see me. I warned him he was taking a chance. I did not change clothes nor put on make-up. If he decided on coming over without an issued invitation, it had to be at his own risk. Take one look and run; it was his option.

He sat on the couch with me and we talked. Finally, I just let him know my concerns. I felt I had some degree of obligation in that he seemed to want a relationship and I was leery. My hope was for a social life – companionship, only. I just blurted out, "You would be much happier with a good, old-fashioned, super-conservative girl, someone who's not bossy or headstrong." I told him all about my five-year plan.

"Are you trying to get rid of me?" he asked.

"If that happens, so be it. I am telling you the truth," I replied.

Then, from his mouth came some of the most surprisingly truthful statements; speaking right to my heart, the truth in them giving me pause.

Each of us is a work in progress. God is not through with any of us… until we draw our final breath.

"You are putting stop signs up at every opportunity. We are not even very far down this road and you are throwing up road blocks. Let's just ease on down the road and see where it leads. By the way, when you do get to a stop sign, you stop and look. You might go to the right, the left, or make a U- turn. You don't have to screech to a halt, or barrel through and crash."

I was astonished. The roadblock analogy is an example of what I have done all my life. I see a few things that I have no answer for, some imperfections and I am ready to pitch the whole thing in the river. The old saying is that I often throw the baby out with the bath water. Having a man that I had known for about three weeks see my classic method of operation and handle it in the way he did was an insight given to me by God, I believe. It was a clear answer to me that this man was worth more time, more exploration, and that there was much more within his character and personality for me to learn.

He asked to take me to my favorite restaurant where we could talk.

"Great. I'll call you." He did and I gave him directions to the restaurant. I was on the right street, but off a wee bit on the exact location.

"It's a good thing I am not driving cross-country with you," he quipped when I drove up. That, too, was one of the messages from God to me. This man learned about me quickly enough and had a way of taking an "oops" situation and making it humorous. No one in his right mind would ever give me a road map. I can hold the map and think I am in charge. But, no one depends on me for directions.

An argument I had with my ex-husband involved directions, compass points, and which way to turn. It capsules my directional dysfunction. So, when a guy is faced with a woman who cannot give simple directions to her favorite restaurant and his reaction is not anger but amusement, he may well be a keeper.

After our dinner date topped with whipped cream and a cherry at *Ben and Jerry's* ice cream store, he kissed me goodbye for the night. It was a good kiss, our first, one that told me this man is respectful. I felt his restraint. I liked everything about that kiss, the feel of his lips included. As soon as I pulled the car out of the parking lot, the cell phone chimed; it was the handsome driver in the other vehicle.

"You know," he softly said, "next time, I am going to get more than that little peck." My heart fluttered, and I smiled. Bring it on.

Chapter 15 – Roadmaps, Roadblocks, and Stop Signs - Reflection:

Respond to these quotes as you contemplate your future.

"The future belongs to those who believe in the beauty of their dreams." – Eleanor Roosevelt

"Forgiveness does not change the past, but it does enlarge the future." - Unknown

Read the following scripture. Next, write a personal reflection about the meaning of each scripture for your life.

1 John 3:18 – *"My little children, let us not love in word, neither in tongue; but in deed and in truth."*

Tart Lesson: It's possible to throw love away.   *Sweet Pleasure: Learn to play it straight.*

Chapter 15 – Roadmaps, Roadblocks, and Stop Signs
Food for Thought:

Ice cream choices can reveal your likelihood of becoming your sweetheart's final lover.

Coffee-ice-cream lovers are said to be dramatic, seductive, flirtatious and are most romantically compatible with strawberry fans. Vanilla gals (emotionally expressive and fond of PDA) melt best with rocky-road guys. And mint-chocolate-chip fans are meant for each other.

If your preference is Vanilla, you are anything but plain. Instead, you are adventurous and fun to be around. Butter Pecan flavor suggests a more traditional person while Rocky Road is not rocky at all, but very eclectic in preferences- a little of this, a little of that.

Hot Spiced Fruit for Ice Cream

This mixture is wonderful served over ice cream or pound cake, and can entice your lover even better than *Ben & Jerry's* fancy flavors-

1 16 oz pear slices (drained)
1 20 oz pineapple chunks (drained)
1 16 oz peach slices
3 heaping T brown sugar

3t cinnamon
2t nutmeg
3t Baking Spices
½ cup butter

Preheat oven to 325 degrees. Melt butter, add brown sugar and spices. Place drained fruit in baking dish.
Pour mixture over fruit and bake uncovered 50-60 min.

CHAPTER 16

Sweeter than Wine

Turn on that record-player memory and listen to Mel Carter. Mel croons of romance and kisses in the moonlight. *Hold Me, Thrill Me, Kiss Me*. Billboard's Top Forty. Hit Parade: 1965.

The lyrics of this pop hit spoke to what I had never experienced, but hoped to find in the man who held my heart: "But they never stood in the dark with you, love, when you take me in your arms and drive me slowly out of my mind."

He held me close, as he leaned against the hood of my car, as I prepared to leave and drive to my house on the other side of town. Standing in the dark with him, being in his arms, and allowing his kisses to mush my brain was seduction that I had never experienced.

When I was in high school, that Mel Carter song was popular. I was involved in a summer romance; we went on picnics and did a lot of kissing. The song by Mel Carter would play on the radio as we were ending our date, parked in my driveway, kissing with our lips tightly closed. That kind of kiss was the only decent way to kiss, as I understood it. Isn't that the way Doris Day and Rock Hudson kissed in *Pillow Talk*, or even the way Sandra Dee and Troy Donahue kissed in *A Summer Place*? The orchestra would crescendo in the introduction to Mel's tribute to the kiss, and my summer heart throb would tell me that was our song. It was a mystery to me how that was true, but every couple should have that one special song. However, as a high-school girl,

I never knew what those lyrics meant, because I had never been driven anywhere by passion...especially not driven "slowly out of my mind."

I have known good kissers. These kisses could accomplish the task, but I don't recall that they were earth-shattering, mind-blowing, or toes-curling. The secret longings of my romantic heart were never touched. I had a very important question on my mind: would I ever find someone who could send love messages to my heart through his kiss?

This current gentleman had asked me to dinner, called me and talked to me for hours. He had been cautious as he held my hand, had not put his arm around me, and had given me a slight kiss after several dates. We had not ignited physical chemistry, but the tension was palpable.

I don't carry the voltage packaged as a Victoria's Secret, pencil thin, drop-dead gorgeous model, but I don't wear orthopedic shoes with a matching Queen Elizabeth handbag, either. I was not looking to be strong-armed or swash-buckled into a lust in the dust, lean-me-over the railing, romance novel kiss. I'd just like to know if there might be potential for anything remotely akin to a swash-buckled, lust in the afternoon, lean-me-over the car hood, romantic kiss.

> *Like Rhett said to Scarlett, "You should be kissed, my dear, and kissed often. And by someone who knows how."*

It was an encouragement when he told me he'd like more than a little kiss, because I had liked his kiss...it pulsated with promise. The texture, pressure, and shape of his lips I remembered. His were not weak lips, tough lips, or wet lips, but just-outright perfect lips. Just the right touch, just the right length of contact - he left us both wanting more. So, when the girlfriends asked, "Has he kissed you?" The answer was yes. "And, is he a good kisser?" What I did not tell them was this: I hope he kisses me again, real soon.

Our evening began routinely enough: shop for a shirt then supper at a local grill. With a great deal of talking and him looking into my eyes, giving me that ultimate turn-on...the gaze, I manage to eat part of a grilled chicken salad.

We returned to where his vehicle was parked and it was time for us to say goodbye for the evening. We sat; we talked and talked. And then the car was quiet. He looked at me and leaned in for "it's been a nice evening, see you later" kiss. I was anticipating this moment and eager to have him close to me – even a hug. I wanted to kiss this man and I wanted him to kiss me. I didn't want to wonder any more.

We leaned into each other, hoping not to impale ourselves on the gearshift console. With skill that only comes from having done this all before, he reached for me and gently grasped my shoulders. I intuitively placed my hand on his chest; our lips came together. The sweetness and tenderness I fell into was a surprise. We lingered and I returned the same depth of response to him, just a little more than before. Then it happened.

While still relishing the soft and tender kiss, he pulled me into an embrace, his strong arms letting me know who would determine the direction this kiss would take. The embrace kindled a quick desire for me to let him know I felt the same. My hand reached instinctively to the back of his neck so I could give him the answer to his question. I gave him equal to what he gave me. That extra intensity in his kiss told me with an affirmative nod the answer to the question of the day. He wrote the book.

My head spun, my heart fluttered, I wanted more. That kiss flew straight out of the chemistry lab with all the bubbling concoctions, hissing steam, and formulas for explosions. I had been kissed by the man I wanted to kiss once more, and forever.

Like Rhett to Scarlett, he could say, "You should be kissed, my dear, and kissed often. And by someone who knows how."

For many months thereafter, we exercised great restraint in order to trudge off to our separate homes and bedrooms. Finding ourselves longing for private time, our kisses blew the roof off bolted down restraint. He was giving me bushel baskets full of all that I needed.

So, why did we continue this frustrating pattern when most adult couples would have been fulfilling the impassioned desire. The answer is this: He knew I was not mentally ready for that step. He recognized the road he'd have to take and while the restraint was frustrating, he wanted the kind of woman before him and was prepared to follow the path. In addition, and perhaps of paramount consideration, I had two sons at home. I was dating in full view of a very critical and highly skeptical audience. Practicing my belief system in full view of my children was clarifying.

Nevertheless, the maestro of the kiss had come along and while teenage years were long past, I found a man whose embrace answered the longings of what I had always wanted to know: As an adult, I received the key, and unlocked the meaning of Mel Carter's lyric, crooned in 1965.

Chapter 16 – Sweeter Than Wine - Reflection:

Married men and women spend many hours with conversation and daily life, far more than with time in the bedroom. So what is it about conversation that builds intimacy and makes any love making more intimately connecting?

Read the following scripture. Next, write a personal reflection about the meaning of each scripture for your life.

Song of Songs, which is Solomon's. 1-2: – *"Let him kiss me with the kisses of his mouth; for thy love is better than wine."*

Song of Songs 2: 6 – *"His left hand is under my head, and his right hand doth embrace me."*

Tart Lesson: Love is certainly more than "the Physical."
Sweet Pleasure: "The Physical" is heavenly with the right person.

Chapter 16 – Sweeter Than Wine - Food for Thought:

Kissing is a prelude to next steps and how well he kisses is a determinant for other strengths, in my way of thinking. Does he play with your lips in response to your playful nibbles? Are his hands in your hair, on your cheek, at the back of your neck? Are his lips soft and pliable, alternately firm and demanding, paired with soft and beckoning? If what you seek is a skilled, passionate lover, you can tell from his kisses.

An often overlooked passion-fruit includes fresh pears. Can you feel the cool, soft texture? Those famous pears shipped everywhere by *Harry and David* are especially sensuous. Sharing a pear with your love can be made even sexier by closing your eyes and feeling the decadent deliciousness fill your mouth. Eat it slowly, so the flavor and the experience will last.

Orange Julius "Love Potion" (it's non-alcoholic)

1-(6 oz) can frozen orange juice	1 cup milk
1-cup water	½ cup sugar
3t Mexican vanilla (Penzey's)	12-15 ice cubes

Put all ingredients into a blender and blend on high for a few seconds until ice is crushed and the mixture is well-blended.

Chapter 17

My Love Story

It's early. It's a Saturday.

The first quietly spoken words I heard were these: "Good Morning, My Darling."

His voice was low and soft. Deep, slow tones, and from my dreamlike stupor, my eyes flew open, because that was a direct hit.

These words traveled straight to my heart and struck like a heat-seeking missile. The hit took my breath away. As I lay in my cozy sheets, eyes closed, a sense of surety overwhelmed me and I was convinced that this man saying good morning to me was the man who wanted to give me the love I had longed for all my life. It was the kind of good morning I could enjoy forever. He should be in my bed, however, and not on the phone.

The love in the letter to the Corinthians is an enduring love, a love that could be between good friends, as well as between the partners in a marriage relationship, regardless of the century. Love is one person desiring the best of all things for the other person. Love is giving first, and getting, later. Love is becoming the right person rather than seeking to find "the one, true right person in the whole wide world." If you will make yourself into the "right" person, good things will follow. Love hopes and believes.

It starts simply, I believe. It starts with a cup of coffee, a glass of tea. It starts with phone calls and long talks, a movie date, a dinner date, and plenty of laughs. Listening, responding, sharing the day. Most couples whose love grows begin that journey by creating friendships. Couples can talk about anything and everything, and frequently do. They can share without fear. Love creeps up on them, softly, on "little cat feet," like the fog in Carl Sandburg's poem. It's through these simple things that the best things begin.

"I think I'm falling in love with you. How can I let you know how deeply I care for you?"

The time we were spending together was stoking the fire and we were speeding, far beyond the limits I had set.

I would have to determine for myself if I wanted to place limits on the growing feelings I had for him.

To myself, I wondered of his desires. I would not go out too far on this limb because my ego is fragile. I have been rejected, also, so if I were to offer love and it were to be refused, that would be quite a wound – it was really risky, even though he is already on his own limb, calling my name.

> *Love creeps up on them, softly, on "little cat feet," like the fog in Carl Sandburg's poem.*

I am trying to determine the best way to either climb this tree, or the best way to get out of the woods altogether.

In all of our days together, I think too much and, I believe, he thinks too little. I am pondering, fighting, listening.

I tried to tell him my feelings that night, standing in my kitchen, but in other words. For some reason, the words, "I love you" were sticking in my throat. I told him, instead, that I cared for him very much, that I adored him.

He basically said, thank you for those kind words, but for me, I need to hear the plain and simple, because that's who I am.

Strange as that may sound, I knew exactly what he meant, but hesitated to put it all on the line, take such a risk, and say the words.

Equally strange, I realized that *I think I am falling in love with you* is a heck of a difference from *I love you*.

A few days later, as I was snuggled in the safe confines of his strong arms, the two of us relaxing together, I placed my hand upon his cheek, looked calmly and sincerely at him, smiling into his soft eyes and said quite clearly, "I do love you." He replied, "I know you do, and I love you, too."

That day and that declaration threw wide the door for a life with just the kind of love I longed for, the love I need. As individual as each of us is, the love we feel and the love that we need is fulfilled in the choice we make for our partner. When the two speak the same language and meet the needs of the other, marriage is easier.

Romantic love, steadfast love, honest love, love that is both vocal and silent – we meet each other's needs in as wonderful an experience as I have ever known.

Chapter 17 – My Love Story - Reflection:

However often you have read I Corinthians:13, read it again. How does it affect your understanding of life today?

Tart Lesson: Affection can deceive, pretending to be love.　　　*Sweet Pleasure: Love abides.*

Chapter 17 – My Love Story - Food for Thought:

Combinations of foods you'd never suspect as being delicious together can include similar combinations in couples. How very different people can become dynamic in their combination suggests similarities to cooking creatively or preparing dishes you would not otherwise consider.

1. Try potato chips inside your sandwich, especially if the sandwich filling is chicken or tuna salad.
2. Add coffee (flavored or regular variety) to vanilla yogurt.
3. Salt on my watermelon slices. What's so different about that?
4. Barbecue pizza is delicious, as is slaw ON a BBQ sandwich, which I think is definitely southern.
5. Have you ever made peanut butter fudge using Velveeta cheese?

Whatever the varying combinations, don't rule out these duos!

Shrimp and Grits (Knock your socks off Classic Southern Duo)

3cups water	3T butter
Salt and pepper	2C shredded sharp cheddar cheese
1 cup instant grits	

(Bring water to boil, add salt and pepper, add grits and cook until water is absorbed, about 20-25 min.
Remove from heat and stir in butter and cheese.)

1lb shrimp, peeled and deveined	Garlic salt
6slices of bacon, chopped	Frozen peppers and onions (spice combo)
3t lemon juice	

(Rinse shrimp and pat dry. Fry bacon in large skillet until browned, drain well. Into this bacon grease add the shrimp. Cook until the shrimp turn pink. Add lemon juice, bacon, other spices and garlic salt. Saute for 3 minutes. Spoon the grits into a serving bowl. Add the shrimp mixture and mix well. _Serve immediately._

Chapter 18

It Was All So Subtle

I was dumbfounded. Though I had timidly confessed my recent understanding to her, she was now adding her knowledge to information I had shared. Hoping she'd say I was mistaken, I was devastated, instead. She confirmed and amplified the story. It's the elephant in the living room that I was afraid to face. I had wondered and asked questions only to have the answers vague enough to satisfy me because I did not want to know the truth.

"Everybody downtown knows… because they wondered if you knew," commented my sweet friend, in a kind, quiet voice, nodding in the affirmative.

We sat opposite each other in deck chairs by her pool. We nursed white wine. Quiet deafened the night.

"He's living one life downtown, at work, and as he drives back to the suburbs, he leaves what he can behind. He stayed as long as he did because you were sick."

I felt slammed into a wall; I did not want to breathe and I closed my eyes.

This is reality, I surmised.

"It's not a secret, except from you," she continued.

Quiet existed no longer.

I don't cry pretty. I look like a done-for, alcoholic prize fighter with puffed eyes and a busted lip. I knew I should not dissolve into a pity-puddle because of the fright I'd look the next day, and the next, ad infinitum. But I did it anyway, because I needed a come-apart. I fell all over myself and cried aloud to voodoo priestesses, begging for tiny, sawed-off straight pins. After a week of applying cold-sore remedy, stye medication, layers of smudge-proof mascara and pancake makeup, I put on my high heels and a pretty shade of lip gloss and prepared to conquer the world.

You probably had this pending disaster sleuthed-out early in the story, wondering when I would discover the truth. You knew instinctively. For whatever reason, I did not. Or, I was in such denial that I convinced myself that such a revelation was not possible. Not him. Not that clever man who had wooed me, wed me, and promised to love me our whole lives through. Nevertheless, it all made some kind of insane sense.

I don't remember when he stopped sleeping with me, but it had been many years since we were intimate. It was all so subtle. He had to work late, read, study, read the paper, watch the late night news, etc. He started to come home late. I went to bed and fell asleep with him not at home. When I awoke, listening for sounds from the living room, I ventured from the bedroom, to find him asleep on the couch or in the chair. I'd wake him. This routine became a standard.

When the older son was in college, the late nights became more blatant and he slept in the vacated bedroom. I started to get phone calls.

One night, I had been awakened by a strange noise and noted that the house was very quiet. I checked on the younger son and then went toward the kitchen. He was not at home. It was almost 2AM. I went back to bed and tried to go to sleep. I had begun to sleep with the phone in the bed, so I could grab it and not wake anyone else.

The phone rang and instead of "Hello," I said, "Where are you?"

It was not he. There was a woman's voice.

She sounded hideous.

"Do you know where your husband is?"

It was not Jake from State Farm.

"Who is this? He's at home," I lied.

"I'm asking you do you know where he is."

I dumbly said again, "Who is this? What are you talking about?"

"Ask him," she said and hung up.

I hung up and immediately pressed numbers for call-back: *69. The phone rang and rang and rang, then switched to that tell-tale FAX buzz. I was startled awake; I could not go back to sleep. I got up and went to the living room, sat down, and waited.

About an hour later, he unlocked the door and walked in. "What are you doing up?" he leveled at me as if I were in the wrong. I told him I had gotten a phone call and had some questions for him. He sat down and said, "OK, who called?" I took him through the conversation and he had an explanation for everything. I cried. He said it was a random phone call by a woman who was a waitress he had offended and she did it out of spite. He tried to cover his escapades like that proverbial French woman who attempts cover with perfumed talc. The story stinks, but I bought it.

Other times he came home after 2AM or sometimes on the weekend, it would be around 6AM. He told me a "bunch of folks from work" met at an apartment and were having some drinks and he fell asleep on the couch and just stayed over. "He didn't want to wake me." How considerate. Again, I accepted it. I was numb….and dumb.

He was leaving home and staying away from home more than ever before and I was allowing it. It was becoming routine. He stayed on the computer when at home and at times would leave to meet his trainer at the gym. I could not find reasons enough to keep him at home, though I tried. If he stayed when I begged, he'd leave later.

I told cover stories. Good at adding a positive spin, I could spin just about anything. Like the time I told the older son that I buried his goldfish with ceremony on the banks of the Great White Waters so it could swim to its mommy and the Fish God when, in fact, I'd flushed it into the sewer.

One day, which in retrospect I think was the last anniversary we shared, we had made plans for dinner. But, work came first and a group of the sales team was to be downtown that evening and into the next day. I became very upset after he had been gone for hours and had not called. I called his pager and got no response. I finally called the hotel and tracked him down. He was there, but it took an Act of Congress to get him to the phone. He vowed that he did not have a room. But, he stayed overnight somewhere on our anniversary.

Since it was our anniversary and we had plans, the younger son was spending the night away from home. I got up early the next morning and drove downtown searching for his car. I did not find it anywhere. I then drove to the bar where he played cards and his car was not there. I had no idea where he was. When he came home that afternoon he said he was at the hotel and that I had just not seen his car and he was upset that I had tried to follow him.

Several friends had gone to dinner at a time after the divorce and we were having dessert, sitting around, talking. They said that I looked troubled and was especially quiet. It was then that I told the friends, "Either he has been having an affair, or he's gay."

> *"We must let go of the life we planned so as to have the life that's waiting for us." -Joseph Campbell*

It was not until then that they said, "What makes you think so?" I told them a lot of things and they shared what they'd learned about the bar he frequented. They had already figured out that he was gay, but had vowed to simply love me through to my own discovery, for if they had told me, I never would have believed it. I had to come to that discovery and voice it.

Prior to the divorce, another revelation surfaced, this time during the battle with ovarian cancer. Mother told me later, after my recovery, that she had answered the phone one night an unidentified female told her, "Your daughter's husband is not where he says he is. He is telling her he is with us, but he is not. I don't know where he is, but I know what he is telling her and it is not true. She needs to know. Maybe not now, but when she gets well, she needs to know."

Much later, after I had recovered and was divorced, Mother told me details she had kept to herself all that time.

According to another friend, he had asked her to be the younger son's God Mother and for them to raise our son if anything happened to him. He also told her that he planned to take our sons to another city where his brother and sister-in-law and other relatives lived. He told her that they would help him raise the children. Knowing him, and his patterns of behavior, he would have left our children with them and gone off in pursuit of his own agenda.

I took pills and wore infused drip pumps to control nausea, but could not control my hair falling out. I could control work, but could not control my world at home. Home was falling apart and I could do nothing about it. I could control my attitude and thought it best not to confront on the behaviors; preserve the status quo. Keep the peace. He left, anyway.

Combing through the wreckage, I realized it had not been so subtle, after all.

Chapter 18 – It Was All So Subtle - Reflection:

"We must let go of the life we planned so as to have the life that's waiting for us." Joseph Campbell

We're just too obsessed with permanence and perfection.

Sometimes mistakes are blessings in disguise, and sometimes seemingly good things cause problems down the road. To beat yourself up for events out of your control is to hold yourself responsible for the universe. We were never supposed to be perfect.

As sinners living together in a fallen world, sin and failure are inevitable.

You might think you are going to find the perfect match but no Christian should live under any such illusion. The Christian, of all people, should be ready to face that fact.

Read the following scripture. Next, write a personal reflection about the meaning of each scripture for your life.

Hebrews 4:15-16 – *"For we have not an high priest which cannot be touched with the feeling of our infirmities; but was in all points tempted like as we are, yet without sin. Let us therefore come boldly unto the throne of grace, that we may obtain mercy, and find grace to help in time of need."*

Tart Lesson: God can forgive homosexuality, alcoholism, abuse, infidelity. Sin is sin, all of it.
Sweet Pleasure: "It wasn't me."

Chapter 18 – It Was All So Subtle - Food for Thought:

"All you need is love. But a little chocolate now and then doesn't hurt."
— Charles M. Schulz

    Myths about chocolate consumption never kept me from indulging. Raised at the knee of a Hershey chocolate bar in heels, I learned the value of a bar in treating everything from a broken heart to a funky mood. Santa believed in chocolate and in sharing it with good little boys and girls. Cupid bought stock in chocolate and must have dipped the tip of his arrows in plenty of it for the world turned, and Chocolate is what makes the world go 'round.

    For improving mood, cardio function, and raising antioxidants levels, a chocolate bar can't be topped. Chocolate truffles, chocolate pie, and chocolate fountains can make even the worst of social events palatable.

    My mother's last request was for a chocolate pie. Having all the ingredients in the kitchen, I baked the pie and we shared it. It was the last thing she asked for and the last thing I was able to do for her, except sit beside her as she drew her last breath.

    Skeptics scream that they'd rather "fall in chocolate" than in love. They must believe because it tastes good, and causes happy-happy, if only for a short while, it must be bad for you, or that love, like chocolate, is from the Devil, as in Devils-food Cake.

    Regardless of the famine or pestilence befalling us, it's fixable – just have some chocolate! You'll feel better!

    Certainly, it's not that easy, but the indulgence can pacify turmoil until your logic returns and you find yourself living again.

Chapter 18 – It Was All So Subtle - Food for Thought:

"The 12-step chocolate program: Never be more than 12 steps away from chocolate."— Terry Moore

"Strength is the capacity to break a chocolate bar into four pieces with your bare hands - and then eat just one of the pieces." — Judith Viorst

"Caramels are only a fad. Chocolate is a permanent thing." — Milton Snavely Hershey

"Life's a box of chocolates, Forrest. You never know what you're gonna get." –Mrs. Gump /*Forrest Gump*

Fudge Pie

3 eggs	pinch of salt
2 squares unsweetened chocolate	½ t Mexican vanilla
1 c sugar	1 pie crust (I use Pillsbury deep dish)
1 stick butter (oleo)	
¼ c flour	

Beat eggs, add sugar, flour, salt, and vanilla.
Mix well. Melt butter, chocolate, and add to egg mixture.
Cook for 20-25 minutes in 350 degree oven in unbaked pie shell.

CHAPTER 19

Life's Tapestry Unravels

Bondage.

Not that kind.

Spiritual bondage. Emotional bondage. Physical bondage in the sense that even the spirit begs for freedom.

The Hebrew people experienced bondage under the army of the Egyptian pharaohs. God freed them with the leadership of Moses who brought them to a land flowing with milk and honey. It took forty-forevers, but God's chosen people were set free from slavery.

No one would ever decree that marriage result in captivity.

Remaining married only because of the Law of Moses or the family's *forever doctrine* sentences the couple to a life of bondage.

Divorce.

The Unraveling. The ultimate come-apart. Or, freedom.

Unlike Penelope who daily unraveled her creation to keep her suitors at bay while Ulysses was fighting his way home, I had no plan to unravel anything. Such a ripping apart of a tapestry that took thirty years to create no one would choose.

College sweethearts. Friends.

Mutual goals. Shared experiences.

My heart broke many times before we married. That happens as couples learn about the power of such love. Desire for deep, intimate fulfillment would result in the ultimate design of God: marriage.

My heart broke many times after we married. The marriage had plenty of good times for a number of years. An observer would never see the troubled waters over which we had built a bridge. If we tried hard enough, we could forget the raging torrent about to send us crashing. He said that he steered the boat enough to keep it off the rocks.

Before our ten year anniversary, a watershed event presented itself. Both of us recognized the turmoil the decision created, but what kind of wife will not support her husband. I voiced my opposition, presented contrary facts and stated my opinion, but loyalty won the day. We went his way.

> *Maybe giving his life to God in the full sense would deter the Devil to such a degree that the various demons would return to the Hell of their origin.*

Ambition. Beliefs. Family. Fun.
Beach. Birthdays. Buddies.
Success. Failure. Celebrations. Sobs.

Linked and meshed into one tapestry, it was marriage woven intricately into a pattern of life. Colors of vibrancy and shades of sadness. Various threads making a story. With only the bright pinks and yellows, the tapestry is unintelligible, undecipherable. Add the darker threads for depth and meaning. When all the threads are woven into the design, the picture is observable. Life insists on all of its colors.

That's why divorce and events leading to it are such travesties. How can life's woven tapestry be split, divided into two equal halves. As Solomon was judging and determining whether to cut the surviving baby into two equal parts, the child's mother halted the ruling. The real mother willed to surrender flesh of her flesh and Solomon saw her truth.

A beautiful sweater or lovely blanket, a museum masterpiece or a piece of living history has been snagged.

"Don't pull that," the admonition is given.

It must be rewoven, but even so, it has become flawed. If the snag, loose thread, is pulled or cut, the entire section unravels and the worked piece is, in the least, damaged or at the most, destroyed.

Memory captures how the relationship grew with the pattern we created. Years of true friendship, linked beliefs and shared events created our life. Then, the fallout of the debilitating years took its final toll.

So, when did it begin to come apart?

He began to bargain with God, attempting to cut a deal. I did not know it was *quid pro quo* at the time. I sensed his misery and turmoil, however. Maybe giving his life to God in the full sense would deter the Devil to such a degree that the various demons would return to the Hell of their origin.

I was placed at the tipping point of the decision to surrender to the ministry; I was opposed and said so. But, he convinced me that he was truly called of God. Imagine denying God's call because of a selfish, world-centered wife. Others expressed their doubts as his decision was such a departure from the original life-path. Ways to serve God abound. Why the pastoral ministry? It was all part of the secret, the rest of the deal.

Gradually I waded into the deep water because the decision gave him peace, and as a result, we were happy: to a point. He knew my misgivings and saw through to my innermost disappointment. He knew I had only sipped the Kool-Aid.

The years spent with initial appointments gained many marvelous experiences and friends for a lifetime. He was happy. We were happy. Joy in serving the Lord and using his personable and charismatic spirit halted some of his restlessness. Business aptitude met spiritual need and it seemed to work. His successful negotiation spilled into our marriage and resulted in pleasant and productive years. Still, I continued to hold uncomfortable feelings. They spilled over many times.

Uneasiness crept into my waking thoughts. I felt something did not fit into this thousand-piece puzzle. Several of the pieces looked like they came from a different box. I could not pinpoint the anomaly for they looked enough similar. I dismissed the misgivings as ridiculous formula thinking. I hammered the pieces into the picture.

The inability to be steady in his career choices haunted him. The bargain was not as successful as he thought. He left the ministry twice, wrangling with emotion and rational thought. He professed the path he'd currently chosen was the one God was placing before him. Ups and downs in both secular and liturgical worlds fueled my reluctance to plunge whole-heartedly into the role of minister's wife. Even as I fought for life itself, my long-time church home and family supported me and the children. I supported his career as an executive wife rather than a clergy-wife. Life at that time was beyond surreal.

I never knew what was coming next. Was he in or out, up or down, happy or miserable, a minister of the Gospel or a master of manipulation.

He became more confounded in his own life and that, too, spilled over into our marriage. Add cancer to that mix and see what happens. The good times began to be overshadowed by calamity: financial, physical, or emotional.

If forced to identify a time when the end began, it was an early end: his decision to enter the ministry. Not the ministry itself, but the supposed deal he was cutting. It was the end result of an internal conflict and turmoil. He saw that life was amiss. His misery created an intangible, vague dissatisfaction for both of us from that point forward. Life's pleasantry camouflaged the underlying discontent.

The long and winding road to divorce began then. It was not paved. Had he not pursued the ministry, we would have remained married for a time, but the upheaval would have led to divorce sooner rather than later. Each life would have taken a different path and who is to say it would have been better? We would have missed the birth of our sons.

We chose marriage.

He knew his truth was the root of his dismay, but acted as best he could the role of husband. This was his Oscar performance. Thing was, I became more confrontational, so blame became the game, and I backed off.

Our end came when the fringes of society taunted, "Come out, come out, Where ever you are!" Non-traditional lifestyles in the guise of *I'm Okay, You're Okay* spun families' normal into chaos. We were not *Okay*. It's hard to play a zero-sum game when all parties stand to lose.

While I wish a change had come from God, a change that would have removed homosexuality from our lives, it did not. The misery we both endured in order to remain married came to an end.

He left; I filed the papers.

The divorce resulted in a total unraveling of everything good and bad, pretty and ugly. The tapestry ripped, snagged, and then lay on the museum's floor in total disarray.

Later, each of us determined to use select threads found in a heap, to weave new lives. Four new designs have been created from the threads of the dismantled original.

To leave it all as destruction would not have acknowledged what lay behind us. For a long time, that tapestry had been a marriage.

He created a new life.

I have made one, too.

So, too, the sons are working on theirs.

Pieces of the old are rewoven along with new threads, but no end result can look like anything worth the salvage effort without God's hand in the process.

Chapter 19 – Life's Tapestry Unravels - Reflection:

No scripture is listed in support of divorce; instead, read these statements derived from my understanding of scripture. Reflect on their meaning for you and your situation, determining through prayer the application to your life.

1. Christ set us free from strict adherence to the old Law. Legalism is superseded by the new law of love, mercy, and grace.

2. Divorce is a failure. Remaining in a failed marriage is a double failure. Failure screams our disaster in relationship, our lack of ability to uphold marriage vows, the ultimate disappointment to the children who will not be brought up in a loving, two-parent home, and the despondency derived from failure to fulfill the dream. Remaining shackled to failure is unfathomable bondage.

3. God forgives. We must forgive our spouse. We must forgive ourselves.

4. Divorce is death. Grief is a natural by-product. Anguish is compounded when one cannot determine how best to grieve.

5. Picture-perfect marriages are perpetuated myths. The ultimate myth-buster is Jesus who lifts up those in pain, those who are broken-hearted, those who are desperate for hope.

Read Romans 8:
God sent His son to give us everlasting life, to give us grace, and to provide the assurance that nothing can separate us from the love of God.

Chapter 19 – Life's Tapestry Unravels - Food for Thought:

No recipe. Recipes combine ingredients.

Instead, it's a quilt project. Not that I have made one. I have a number of quilts and fabric remnants belonging to various loved ones within the family, pieces cut from another whole, pieces for a quilt. Mother made a "crazy quilt" from fabrics identifiable as to which skirt, dress, or slacks someone in our family had worn, items she had sewn with love.

New quilts are sewn from new designer fabrics. A quilt fashioned from remnants, or in this case, four quilts made from the original wedding ring interlocking quilt pattern, would be quite an undertaking. Should you attempt to create four new masterpieces, consider what pieces of the older, ruined item will be placed within the new designs. Consider, too, the placement of the old fabric, because fresh, newly woven fabric representing all that is alive and well must be the majority. Some of the old fabric may be dry-rotted and must be discarded entirely.

An entire analogy is possible.

You get the picture.

Tart Lesson: Taking forward too much of the old and allowing it to dominate the new pattern ruins the new creation.

Sweet Pleasure: Incorporating vintage understanding into a new design salutes what is past and opens creative possibilities.

CHAPTER 20

Holding On or Letting Go

The experts are right. For a woman, at least, it takes about one year for every five years of marriage to deal with all the issues and pains of the past. Only when that is done can a woman place both feet squarely in the present and bring with her the good lessons she has learned and not the soggy baggage of old wounds and weighty resentment. It should be that way for men, too, but men become lonesome and they cannot, or will not, wait any healthy length of time to remarry. Hopefully, you will not be the rebound marriage, because that one is surely doomed to failure; he has not dealt at all with the issues of the train wreck.

Some of the issues I had to deal with included beliefs about my femininity, my own desires. I had to deal with the issues of finances, trust and honesty. I had to deal with expressing my feelings and learning to hold myself and others accountable for their behavior. I vowed not to be an enabler again, vowed to say how I felt and if an argument was the result, then there would be one. I would not hold back.

"When one door of happiness closes, another opens; but often we look so long at the closed door that we do not see the one which has been opened for us." – Helen Keller

I did not realize that I was not sleeping at night. If my ex-husband did not come in until quite late, I was subconsciously awake until then. If I chose to get up and confront him on the situation, that meant I had fewer hours of sleep until the alarm sounded.

When I finally found the bank statements, I discovered where the money had been going. I found evidence of credit/debit card use at bars around town, but primarily at one bar in the center-city area.

And, it was not until almost six years later that the real truth surfaced. When I learned the absolute truth about the shell of a marriage and resulting divorce, I finally knew it was not me. Every doubt I had about my own femininity, my own sex-appeal vanished. Every humiliating night of rejection, every tear of mortification evaporated. There was never a single thing I could have done to save the marriage. I had been drowning in a gulf of ambiguity.

I was busy trying to save a marriage that had no hope. I was doing what I thought I should do. Holding on was my action. I still think I should have done all those things – tried with all my heart, soul, being to save that marriage and make it what God wanted it to be. I couldn't save it, though. While God was laying the foundation for survival and future success, I was clinging to the past.

My sons have told me that my holding on was misplaced concern for them, that they and I would have been just fine had my action been a bold one. Fear immobilized me. Trust God, yes, and in doing so, act to preserve your self-worth and dignity.

Change is scary and marriage vows are sacred: "For better or worse, for richer or poorer, in sickness and in health, until death do us part." I thought we were experiencing a great deal of worse. After emotional survival from a crumbling marriage, one in total disarray for almost ten years, I still believed that my illness had been primarily responsible for the missing pieces. Blaming myself was far easier than learning the truth.

Time came to let go.

Looking toward the future with this man I came to love, I learned that I did not want to spend any more time than necessary away from him. I did not want a dating, significant other relationship. I wanted a come home from work, share the day, sleep together at night and wake up beside one another every morning relationship. The sooner, the better. It was a surprise.

As the weeks and months progressed to our wedding day, our mutual desire and accompanying satisfaction struck an even deeper and more euphoric accord. With our vows came the sense of oneness experienced by men and women who commit through God and His marriage principles. No longer would we separate each night to sleep alone.

As our months have progressed to years, our passion for each other has increased and our deep love has produced an intimacy reserved for husbands and wives. His openness and patience kindled what had remained untouched within me. This man would be all my "good nights" and my welcoming, "Good Morning, My Darling."

I am glad I found a man who tells me how lovely and beautiful a woman he sees before him, how sexy I am. He thanks me for bringing so much good into his life. I found a lover who gazes directly into my eyes and locks in with intimate knowledge, seeing past the loved-off fur.

I thank God daily, not only for my life, but for restoring in me the belief in myself and the capacity for a committed, loving relationship with a flawed, down-to-earth, real-life man, one whose fur splotches appear even more tattered than mine.

Chapter 20 – Holding On or Letting Go - Reflection:

Read the following scripture. Next, write a personal reflection about the meaning of each scripture for your life.

Matthew 6:8b, 31-34 - *"For your Father knoweth what things ye have need of before ye ask him. Therefore, take no thought, saying, What shall we eat: or, What shall we drink: or, Wherewithal shall we be clothed? For after all these things do the Gentiles seek: for your heavenly Father knoweth that ye have need of all these things. But seek ye first the kingdom of God, and his righteousness; and all these things shall be added unto you. Take therefore no thought for the morrow: for the morrow shall take thought for the tings of itself. Sufficient unto the day is the evil thereof."*

Choose several or all quotes listed. They were gleaned from multiple sources and are valid in a variety of ways. Reflect in writing how the quotes you have chosen can affect your life and the life of your family.

1. "Regret and fear are twin thieves that rob us of today." Robert Hastings

2. "The gem cannot be polished without friction, nor man perfected without trials." Chinese proverb

3. "Some people think that it's holding on that makes one strong; sometimes it's letting go." Unknown

4. "Pain is inevitable. Suffering is optional." -M. Kathleen Casey

5. "I don't miss him; I miss who I thought he was." –Unknown

6. "The future belongs to those who believe in the beauty of their dreams." -Eleanor Roosevelt

7. "It is not death that a man should fear, but he should fear never beginning to live." -Marcus Aurelius (121-180)

8. Relationships are like glass. Once they are broken, it's better to leave them that way than to hurt yourself trying to put them back together.- Unknown

Tart Lesson: Life is messy, sometimes ugly.   Sweet Pleasure: God can turn your life upside down.

Chapter 20 – Holding On or Letting Go - Food for Thought:

When life gets overwhelming and you feel powerless to do anything about it, get thyself into the kitchen! Chop it, blend it, pound on it, create it and then, enjoy it.

Start with the marvelous Pizza to nurture power. Dice some vegetables and cheeses for toppings. Blend ingredients into a sauce. Find some spices that you enjoy and use them to invigorate your pizza. Blend the dough, or use the prepackaged type. Pound on it, kneed it, roll it and then, if you feel brave, throw it around. Your accomplishment will be worth your effort.

Unfortunately, your life is not altogether as simple as a pizza. It could be a challenge to order "life" as we order a pizza. "I'll have the Life Special with a good job, two kids, a dog, and a spacious house in the suburbs." God is not a pizza delivery man and your petitions are not orders for "extra wardrobe, fancy car, and stuffed pantry." Your life cannot be ordered and delivered in "30 minutes or less." Some people pray that way and fall into disillusionment when it does not work out like that.

We order pizza at the last minute: "Just order a pizza." We have no ongoing relationship with the person at Speedy Delivery Pizza. The only time we call is when we want…a pizza. Has your prayer life become similar to pizza ordering?

Fruit Pizza (Many ingredients, delicious by themselves, but much better when combined into one incredible dessert.)

1 pkg refrigerator sugar cookie dough	1 8oz pkg cream cheese
	1 c pineapple chunks
1 c banana slices	1 kiwi sliced
1 c strawberries sliced	1 t vanilla

1 jar Orange *Smuckers* or other fancy jam or jelly, microwave slightly to soften

Slice cookie dough and press together on a greased pizza pan. Bake at 350 degrees for 15 min. Let cool. Combine cream cheese, vanilla, sugar and beat 'til smooth.

Spread on cooled cookie.

Arrange fruit in rings on top.

Pour sauce over fruit evenly. Chill and serve in slices like pizza.

Chapter 21

"Marriage is not for me."

"Marriage is not for me," said the young husband, as I read the story on Facebook. He shared a story that led the reader through to his discovery that marriage was not "for him," alone. He shared that he learned to think not about himself but about his wife. When she does the same for him, a long term marriage is possible for this couple.

> I'll buckle up my boots and pull on my big girl britches.
> It's going to be one heck of a ride.
> It's called a real marriage.
> This is not moonlight and magnolias, Scarlett. Atlanta is burning.
> My hair needs cut and color. My hubby needs a shave. He's been working in the man cave and he stinks. The goldfish died and I burned the dinner. He has the remote in one hand, his cellphone on the chair arm, and the computer in his lap. I'm reading…or writing…or both.
> We mess up.
> Demonstrative with affection, dependable in every way, solid and secure, able to leap tall buildings in a single bound: I craved these attributes. He is solicitous, with a heart for helping and caring, a tenderness I have never witnessed in a man.
> The struggles of his life shed light on why his personal relationships have been difficult.

Read about it every day, throughout America. Read about it here. Now, it's personal.

I made a decision to marry the person I loved and the person who provided for me the security I needed. I hoped my husband could teach my sons some valuable lessons, and be a strong male role model. That would be a bonus. They have a father and children who are beyond the teen years will leave the house, eventually, and live their lives as they choose. So, I made the decision to marry to fulfill my needs and desires.

I discovered more information about his children and the fundamentalist preachers that created holy wars for his family. As all parents do, he did what he believed was right at the time. It was too harsh, however, for too many years. He is reaping what he has sewn with family members.

My husband has said he's learned more about parenting within the last 10 years, than he ever knew when he needed to know it. He had no model for good parenting and was prone to anger and absolute authority. This is not a good combination.

He is also learning more about relationships as the years progress and has asked forgiveness from all the children. Too much happened, though, for Barney sing-a-longs and group hugs. Our various backgrounds carry similar values but quite different styles.

> *I pray that my love and I have shaken the dust from our feet and turned our faces toward the future.*

So, here is the situation. It's every couple's situation.

We are adults. Two people from different backgrounds, and we are married, as Rebecca Ward has explained in her book about surviving marriage while retaining sanity (33). Had I said, "No," even though I loved him, he would have moved on, as I would have. He knew I was a risk, he has said. There is no way to know what would have happened next for either of us had our decisions been different.

Qualities such as fidelity, honesty, trustworthiness: I looked for them. When I found them, I put some of his past mistakes aside. We all have poor habits from the past.

When I got all the information I needed, I knew that this man loved me and wanted to do nothing in his life but please me and make me happy. I was free to love him, and let him know that I welcomed him into my life, all of him, and that I looked forward, not backward. Love can be used as salve to wounds and can heal broken lives.

Fully aware that dating behaviors stop when marriage begins, he exhibited enough of the qualities I longed for in a man and has provided the security and affection I craved.

This was my prayer: Dear Heavenly Father, Allow me to put down the measuring stick. I pray that my love and I have shaken the dust from our feet and turned our faces toward the future, and that we have been placed together for our mutual benefit and God's pleasure.

What do we do now?

A gem cannot be perfected without friction.

I provide the sandpaper for his rough edges. He discourages my enabling behaviors.

God help us now, is my prayer.

Now, it's time to go to work, to have a marriage.

Marriage is work. Beautiful work. A worthy work. Long term marriage is work for a long time, as in "'til death do us part."

One of our strengths is the ability to talk. We can chatter, share, or be quiet. We disagree, debate, act and react. Each of us needs to be a better listener. We know we are entirely different individuals, that we will never be alike (hallelujah!). We respect our differences, for the most part.

As addressed previously, we who profess Christianity should know before everyone else that no one is perfect. Remember that I was seeking the next "Mr. Wrong" who could be Mr. Right for me. I also mentioned how I clung with bloody fingernails to the dream of an intact marriage. That did not work, but it was worth the effort. That's what everyone should do, in my opinion: hold on until someone pries your fingers loose or stomps your hands into reality.

Our big hurdle is learning each other's communication styles and making a working style for us. Blending. What worked for him then does not work with me, now. And vice-versa. We talk and talk and talk but must learn to communicate better.

As I've struggled through writing this chapter, I come to the same point every time. Regardless of what story I was preparing to share, the end result was this realization: marriage is work. Some days, it's hard work. So, even if someone might relate to an illustration or instance, the reader might focus on that one thing and miss the point, as I could, myself. Regardless of your struggle, the continuous work within a marriage is worth it.

His past, my past. His way of acting, reacting and my way must come to an "our way." Frank Sinatra crooned that he did it "His Way." I am going to live my life for my husband and for me. I will compromise or hold fast, as appropriate. No one, in my estimation, can flourish within a long-term marriage if he/she thinks only "My Way."

With appreciation for who each one of us has become, I can be myself. He can do the same. Nevertheless, compromise lives. According to Rebecca Ward (How to Stay Married Without Going Crazy, 2012), "You are married. You are adults. You cannot have both cookies" (73).

Chapter 21 – "Marriage Is Not for Me" - Reflection:

Going through this life sharing cookies with a partner is far better than navigating it alone. To make the journey with someone you love is worth the work.

Write your response to these quotes as they relate to working hard in a long-term marriage:

"I've never tried to block out the memories of the past, even though some are painful. I don't understand people who hide from their past. Everything you live through helps to make you the person you are now." –Sophia Loren

"Forgiveness does not change the past, but it does enlarge the future." Unknown

Tart Lesson: The Past can haunt a couple.
Sweet Pleasure: Lessons about who we are as individuals come from the Past. From our past we create a marriage for our Future.

Chapter 21 – "Marriage Is Not for Me" - Food for Thought:

I wish to share that I appreciate Rebecca Fuller Ward's <u>How to Stay Married Without Going Crazy-</u>Second Edition, 2013, WordsWorth Books & Co. (first edition, January, 2000).

    I read Mrs. Ward's book in one sitting. Her straight-forward language and advice are right on the money. Like she needs me to say that, with her credentials and experience! I felt a connection with her and her book.

    With appreciation to her, allow me to share this recipe:

<u>Crazy Cake</u>
    Place all ingredients into a bowl:

1 cup sugar	1 ½ cup sifted flour-with ½ t salt
1 egg	and 1 t baking powder, ½ t
½ cup milk,	baking soda
½ cup cocoa	½ cup boiling water
½ cup shortening	1 t vanilla.

Beat for 3 min.

Bake in prepared muffin tins in slow oven (325 degrees) for 30 min.

<u>Frosting:</u>

1 cup sugar	3 T cream
3 T cocoa	1 t vanilla
3 T butter	

Cook 5-10 minutes or until it coats the spoon. Add 8 marshmallows and beat until thick.

Conclusion

Discovering *Sunrise in a Lemon Sky*

If we open ourselves to God's direction and listen to Him and follow the gentle prodding of our hearts, He will lead us to a new life – one better than we ever hoped. We must find encouragement in the power of God to direct our lives. Whatever He has waiting for us, it will be revealed in His time, in His way, and through His plans. We know it will be all we ever needed, and more.

He expects us to follow His lead and act on Faith. Remember Noah.

What he has done and continues to do for me, He can and will do for persons who desire God's activity in their lives. Ask Him, trust Him to give; listen and watch for His answers. Then act on what is revealed. Remember Joseph's dreams.

A trip with my ex-husband prior to our marriage revealed to me a clue to his behavior pattern: arguments and two double beds. He slept in his, I in mine. He never crossed the center line. The exciting expectation of a passionate romantic weekend crashed. He was an honorable gentleman.

I have two marvelous sons. They came to me as all children come, from God. Yet, my children arrived in my heart and into my arms by way of adoption. When I was crying and begging, and praying and arguing with God, He was smiling down on me saying, "In due time and in My way." He provided two young women an answer to their prayers at the same time He answered mine. It was best that I not risk the genetic danger in misaligned chromosomes, especially as I grew older.

I survived ovarian cancer. The silent killer, the most deadly form of cancer for women was eradicated from my body. Prayer and modern miracles of medicine, God's hand on the hand of the surgeon and in the protocols designed by the oncologist saved my life. My friends, family, colleagues, steadfast girlfriends, and countless prayer warriors rescued me. They lifted me from certain death and saved my children, too. There had been symptoms, as far back as February prior to the discovery and diagnosis in June. The dog's paw on my abdomen created sharp pain. Hmmm, I thought. Tampons had become difficult to insert, requiring an odd angle. Hmmm, that's strange. Monthly cycles were sickening, with bile-filled indigestion and diarrhea. I explained away these anomalies.

When I first began to ponder that God had truly saved my life from a horrible, deadly disease, I believed it was for the good of my children, only. And, while I do not pass an opportunity to thank God daily, hourly for that miracle, and while I still believe my children to be a primary reason that I am alive, I now believe that God worked within all the scenarios to save my life for me, as well.

New meaning to hymns came to me bringing celebration with every line: *Great is Thy Faithfulness*…moment by moment new blessings I see…all I have needed Thy hands have provided, Great is Thy faithfulness, Lord unto me; *Because He Lives*…I can face tomorrow, Because He lives, all fear is gone…; *It Is Well With My Soul*…When sorrows like sea billows roll…Thou hast taught me to say, It is well, it is well with my soul.

Through divorce and financial worries, God gave me answers about His ability to help me through every trial. Just when I thought my life might turn around when my health was restored, another chunk of my sky fell. The demise of a thirty year marriage shook my core. God let me see clearly what marriage had been, and he had plans to give me another chance at discovering happiness in marriage. And, even living single, I never worried about money again.

I was forced to acknowledge that my marriage was ruined almost in totality because the man in the equation is a homosexual. Yes, there were clues there, too. I could not get the words out of my mouth to level the accusation or confront him with my fears. In part, I was grateful to learn that all the doubts I had about my sex appeal and femininity were misplaced. It's why I could never figure him out – his complexity was backwards to me. When I thought I had it understood or thought I knew what he wanted from me, it would backfire. I was in a quandary because the confusing situation is contrary to what I believe about God's Universe. He told me he could not be my knight in shining armor. He had a secret; he chose me because I was quick to believe and ready to trust. Through my behavior, I reminded him daily of who he was not; I begged him to be who he vowed that he was. He bargained with God, but when that did not work, he fell into cahoots with the Devil.

It must be misery to feel trapped by such an enormous secret as the one he kept for so many years. Both of us were set free when he left. The complexity of the situation will never be totally smoothed, as children are a part of the story. We all are forever different.

What resulted destroyed a dream and changed everyone within our family. For thirty years we lived in a marriage held together during the final ten years by sheer willpower. This was the time society opened the closet door and secrets tumbled out.

While each of us can give reasons for the demise of the marriage, can acknowledge the good years, there is no denying the situation was horrible, hurtful, and crushing. My heart healed, however, and desired to love again.

Appearing on my radar was a man who understands who I used to be and who I have become. He appeared out of nowhere…a persistent blip. He was in no place and in no way anyone I would have found on my own, in my own very limited knowledge and experience. This man was surprised to find me, also.

His past did not include you, but from this point on, his future will.

For almost forty years, we had lived somewhat parallel lives, in locality and in experiences, crossing paths for twenty years. We grew up in the 1960s, so no explanation is necessary when a particular "Oldie Goldie" plays on the Sirius XM radio. Our differences are definite, but we balance each other well.

Though I shed a tear occasionally over his past and mine, I am happy to be cherished, adored, and loved in the most wonderful of ways because he knows that I am not only the last, but the best. God answered both of us in ways neither of us had imagined.

My wish for everyone is God's Peace. We should cast our burdens upon Him, and trust Him to lead. He is Wonderful Counselor, Mighty God, Everlasting Father, Prince of Peace (Isaiah 9:6). In experiencing the Savior, Jesus, our Lord, we experience God.

From William Wordsworth's ***Ode on Intimations of Immortality***, I share Wordsworth's final lines in summation:
"Thanks to the human heart by which we live,
Thanks to its tenderness, its joys and fears,
To me the (smallest) flower that blows can give
Thoughts that do often lie too deep for tears."

I have learned that some of the most intimate moments are in conversation and silences. Even honest argument is emotionally intimate. Intimacy of all kinds translates with a satisfying physical relationship, which is critical for men and women, alike. God created this desire within us and provided marriage as the most private, personal, intimate fulfillment.

In long-time marriages, couples have discovered how to satisfy each other in a variety of ways. Whatever it is that is satisfactory for the couple is wonderfully perfect. Find your passion with your mate, and enjoy!

CONCLUSION – Discovering Sunrise in a Lemon Sky - Reflection:

Read the following scripture. Next, write a personal reflection about the meaning of each scripture for your life.

Galatians 5: 22-23 – "But the fruit of the Spirit is love, joy, peace, longsuffering, gentleness, goodness, faith, Meekness, temperance; against such there is no law."

John 14: 27 - "Peace I leave with you, my peace I give unto you; not as the world giveth, give I unto you. Let not your heart be troubled, neither let it be afraid."

Psalm 30: 4-5 : - "Sing unto the Lord, O ye saints of his, and give thanks at the remembrance of his holiness. For his anger endureth but a moment; in his favour is life; weeping may endure for a night, but joy cometh in the morning."

"Turn your face toward the sun and the shadows will fall behind you." ~ Maori Proverb

CONCLUSION – Discovering Sunrise in a Lemon Sky
Food for Thought:

Recipe books have their own versions of a recipe that is so perfect, so wonderful, so fulfilling that some have coined the expression, it is "better than sex."

Recipe: "Better Than Sex" Cake! *(According to Billy Joel, a peanut butter & jelly sandwich is more desirable than bad sex.)*
    Warning: Recipe contains Chocolate & Pecans

Put all these ingredients into one bowl and mix:

German Chocolate Cake Mix	1 c. Vegetable Oil (Wesson or Crisco)
1 pkg Instant Chocolate Pudding	
1 12 oz. pkg. Mini-Chocolate Chips	4 Eggs
	3c. chopped pecans
1 8 oz. container Sour Cream	

Pour mixture into prepared BUNDT PAN.
Bake at 350 degrees for 1 hr 15 min.
Cut yourself a SLAB of this cake when it cools a little bit.
Consider adding Ice Cream to the warm cake.

To bring this memoir to a close, I offer a final family recipe and blessing:

May your sunrises be filled with life's zest.
Take the tart with the sweet, combining them into a deliciously fulfilling life, as God and you have made it so.

LEMON ICEBOX PIE (courtesy of my "grand"-mother who secreted many recipes into her handwritten cookbook. Really good recipes were noted as "Grand!")

1 14oz can Eagle Brand milk	3 egg yolks
½ cup Lemon Juice	1 8" graham cracker crust or pre-baked pie shell
1 t grated lemon zest	

In medium bowl, combine milk, lemon juice, and zest.
Blend in the egg yolks.
Pour into cooled crust.

Meringue:
3 egg whites
¼ t cream of tartar
¼ c sugar

Preheat oven to 325 degrees. Beat egg whites with cream of tartar until soft peaks form.
Gradually beat in the sugar until peaks are stiff. Spread over filling. Seal to edge of the crust.
Bake for 12-15 minutes, or until meringue is golden brown.

Epilogue

It's exhausting to write a book such as this one and expend emotional energy reliving years of turmoil, thrills and joys. It's also exciting, considering the potential for good to come from it. It is my hope that individuals, women's groups, or book clubs might explore the *Reflection* sections and share insights and experiences. Regardless of the trials in life, we can survive the sting.

Recently, I was released from the Cancer Clinic to which I had been attached for over 20 years. It was this clinic and their oncologists and surgeons whose treatments saved my life. They are the most remarkable, Godly people, treating each patient as an individual. The clinic, the doctors and nurses became another family for me. To be told that a regular gynecologist could care for me now surprised me, for I thought I'd always be under the specter of a cancer diagnosis. There is comfort in constant vigilance against cancer's ugly image. Time had been sufficient, though, and I was ready. My gynecological oncologist made sure I had doctors lined up for preventive health-care and dismissed me. After 20 years! Wow!

Both sons, hearts of my heart, are employed and happy. They have told me that had I divorced sooner, they would have understood and applauded my courage. We would have been just fine.

Family and friends have continued to surround me with love and support. I explored social media and have enjoyed connecting with friends in extended circles. My writing colleagues encourage and support these efforts.

Another major health crisis surfaced this year. It was not related to any previous disease. Nevertheless, a tumor had been growing inside my heart. It was a benign atrial myxoma. An episode of congestive heart failure sent me to the Emergency Room, and directed by God, one person after another met my needs. Each one contributed to the successful path to surgery, and ultimately, complete wellness. God once again reached into my life and decisions of others. My brother and his wife, my sons, girlfriends, pastors were at my side. My husband is cemented as my hero. He takes care of me and is especially protective

My husband and I are still learning each other, appreciating every day. Conflict arises for we are very different individuals. Perhaps another memoir will continue my story. As everyone learns, we are either in the midst of a dilemma, coming out of one, or heading smack-dab into another.

I have never been a syrupy sweet girl. I vowed, however, to find opportunity to view the rocky circumstances of life in a different light. "Making lemonade out of lemons" may be worthy goal, but that's just not me. I have found both sweet and sour within my life and my hope is that the authenticity of this memoir will speak truth to you. When God speaks, listen. Then, act.

Thank you for reading my story; writing is has been a clarifying experience.

Index to "Food for Thought"

Appetizers, Beverages, Extra Treats

Hot Spiced Fruit Bake	Chapter 15
Lemon Curd (Sauce)	Chapter 13
Orange Julius	Chapter 16
Salted Pecans	Chapter 4

Salads and Soups

Broccoli and Cheese Soup	Chapter 5
Cornbread Salad	Chapter 9
Kickin' Chicken Vegetable Soup	Chapter 6
Millionaire Salad	Chapter 11

Main Dishes

Hot Chicken Salad	Chapter 12
Magic Meat Loaf	Chapter 2
Shrimp n' Grits	Chapter 17

Desserts

    Better Than Sex Cake   Conclusion
    Coconut Pie   Chapter 10
    Crazy Cake   Chapter 21
    Date Nut Cake   Chapter 1
    Death by Chocolate   Chapter 7
    Easy Pound Cake   Introduction
    Flower Pot Dessert   Chapter 8
    Fruit Pizza   Chapter 20
    Fudge Pie   Chapter 18
    Inside-Out Cake   Introduction
    Lemon Icebox Pie   Conclusion
    Pineapple Upside Down Cake   Chapter 14
    Signature Lemon Cake   Chapter 13

Recipe for a Happy Marriage   Chapter 4

-The Symphony-
These things do we earnestly desire:

A clear vision of life, that with gracious and kindly
hearts we may share both joy and sorrow
and bring into living reality
the Sisterhood of women.

An appreciation of real merit and worth, steadfastness of soul,
that without bitterness or defeat we may encounter misfortune
and with humility meet success.

These things, O Lord, help us to instill within our hearts
that we may grow in courage and graciousness and peace.
Written in 1924 by Helen Willis Lynn, Alice
Matthews, and Almira Cheney.

"Do all the good you can. By all the means you can. In all the
ways you can. In all the places you can. At all the times you
can. To all the people you can. As long as ever you can."
~ attributed to John Wesley.

About the Author

The author of <u>Sunrise in a Lemon Sky</u> used the pen name E. J. Gordon. While dear friends, family, and associates know the story intimately, the author wishes to give some privacy to those who desire it. She has lived through a number of crisis events and is quick to point out that her experiences are not necessarily worse than those of others, but they were earth-shattering to her. The author uses an authentic voice tempered with humor.

Her undergraduate degree is in English and she has participated in writers' retreats, seminars, and classes. Writing several blogs, she entertains friends and keeps them updated through her stories. The ability to find the right phrase or the best word is a daily challenge.

Her ability to tell a good story makes her book come alive. The authenticity has moved friends to fresh tears. She has experienced God's hand in her life and learned how to look for and listen to Him in daily activity.

She is living in a small town in her home state with her husband, as both have retired. The couple works in volunteer efforts, travels, explores genealogy, and embraces the sunrises of every day.